To Marjorie – DAVID B. WILLIAMS

To Brad, Henry, and Elliot – JENNIFER OTT

WATERWAY

THE STORY OF SEATTLE'S LOCKS AND SHIP CANAL

DAVID B. WILLIAMS, JENNIFER OTT, AND THE STAFF OF HISTORYLINK

HistoryLink and Documentary Media

Seattle

WATERWAY THE STORY OF SEATTLE'S LOCKS AND SHIP CANAL

HistoryLink
1411 4th Avenue, Suite 803
Seattle, WA 98101
(206) 447-8140
admin@historylink.org

First Edition
Printed in China

Produced by Documentary Media LLC
books@docbooks.com
www.documentarymedia.com
(206) 935-9292

Authors: David B. Williams, Jennifer Ott, and the staff of HistoryLink
Editor: Judy Gouldthorpe
Book Design: Marilyn B. Esguerra, Philips Publishing Group
Production Assistant: Amelia von Wolffersdorff
Editorial Director: Petyr Beck, Documentary Media LLC

ISBN: 978-1-933245-43-0

Distributed by the University of Washington Press
uwapress@uw.edu
(206) 543-4050

_____
Library of Congress Cataloging-in-Publication Data

Names: Williams, David B., 1965- author. | Ott, Jennifer, 1971- author. |
    HistoryLink (Firm), author.
Title: Waterway : the story of Seattle's locks and ship canal / by David B.
    Williams, Jennifer Ott and the staff of HistoryLink.
Description: First edition. | Seattle, Washington : Documentary Media LLC,
    2017. | Includes bibliographical references and index.
Identifiers: LCCN 2016046693 | ISBN 9781933245430
Subjects: LCSH: Lake Washington Ship Canal (Seattle, Wash.)--History.
Classification: LCC TC625.L5 W55 2017 | DDC 386/.4709797772--dc23
LC record available at https://lccn.loc.gov/2016046693

CONTENTS

INTRODUCTION   7

The McClellan Myth
Other Canals

CHAPTER 1 GEOLOGY AND NATIVE HISTORY   19

Native Villages and Historic and Modern Towns

CHAPTER 2 EARLY HISTORY: 1854-1892   35

Coal and the Canal
Army Corps of Engineers
Chinese Labor Contractors

CHAPTER 3 ROUTING AND FUNDING   51

Eugene Semple
McGilvra, Greene, and Burke
Hiram Chittenden
1909 State Shore Land Improvement Fund

CHAPTER 4 BUILDING THE CANAL:
1909-1917   71

Dam Bursts
Fremont Cut
Making Strong Concrete
Workers
James Bates Cavanaugh
Notable Early Boats Through the Locks
Other Locks
The Full Cut and Cost

CHAPTER 5 CHANGING SHORELINE,
CHANGING REGION   101

Fishermen's Terminal
Military Installations
Parks Along Lake Washington in Seattle

CHAPTER 6 ENVIRONMENTAL CHANGE   113

Teredos in Salmon Bay
Boats Run Into Submerged Forest
Saltwater Incursion
Smelt and *Daphnia*

CHAPTER 7 THE LIFE OF THE CANAL   129

Emergency Dam
Other Washington Canals
Cedar River Diversion
Pedestrian Crossing
Opening Day and Crew Races
Herschel, Hondo, and Steelheads
Memorials at the Locks

SHIP CANAL TIMELINE   150

ACKNOWLEDGMENTS   152

BIBLIOGRAPHY   154

PHOTO CREDITS   157

INDEX   158

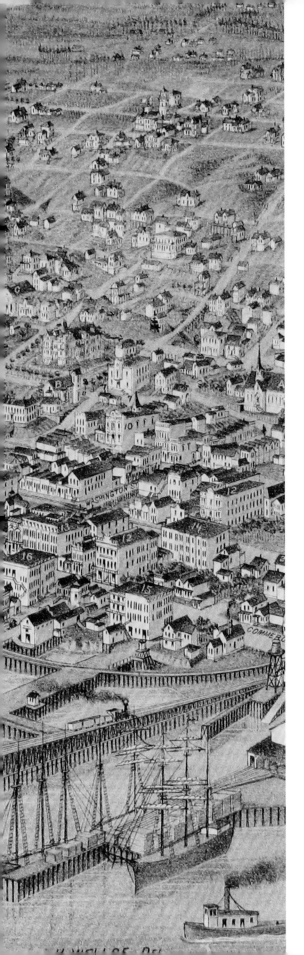

Introduction

In the early 20th century, Seattle was a city based on waterways, with working waterfronts on Elliott Bay, Lake Washington, Lake Union, and Salmon Bay. Canoes, rowboats, steamers, sailing ships, fishing boats, and passenger ferries plied the waters carrying everything from coal to people to wheat. And yet in this maritime city, with its eye on a future based in manufacturing and shipping, the existing waterways fell short. Small, low-lying strips of land separated the saltwater harbor from the freshwater lakes and the lakes from each other. Moving between the inland waters and Puget Sound required multiple portages (hauling watercraft or cargo between bodies of water) or negotiating the shallow, unpredictable Duwamish River. To unlock the full bounty and potential of the region, the waterbodies needed to be connected via a waterway, and city leaders would spend more than 60 years making that happen.

As early as 1884, the Seattle waterfront was crowded with piers. Promoters hoped that by opening a waterway to the lakes, miles of undeveloped shoreline free of tides and ship-damaging marine organisms would stimulate development and industry.

Thomas Mercer was the first to call for the joining of the lakes and Puget Sound in 1854, when Seattle was only three years old. Most of the town's 100 to 150 settlers clustered in small cabins around today's Pioneer Square. Henry Yesler's mill was just getting established, a handful of ships tied up to his wharf each year, and Portland, the nearest city, was several days away by boat. But the first non-Native settlers did not come to Puget Sound to get away from it all; they came to build a city that would be at the crossroads of global trade routes.

The ship canal was part of the plan to open the regional waterways to maritime commerce and make it possible to tap the region's vast natural resources. In the days of horsepower, King County's hills posed significant obstacles to commerce, and Mercer's corridor between salt water and freshwater, as generations of Coast Salish people had known, could serve as a highway to transport people and goods. In the process, Seattle would evolve from a frontier outpost into a "world-class city."

Some of this vision came to fruition. Seattle has become a major port city, and for several decades there was barely a foot of unoccupied shoreline on Lake Union and Salmon Bay because of the maritime industry and moorages lining the banks. These include the North Pacific fishing fleet, which has been estimated to be worth $6 billion annually, as well as shipbuilding, ship repair, salvaging operations, foundries, and tugboat services. Although Lake Washington saw less development, it still had significant industries, from Boeing in Renton to Lake Washington Shipyards at Kirkland. More than any other maritime event before or since, the opening of the Lake Washington Ship Canal and Hiram M. Chittenden Locks transformed the waterways and shorelines of Seattle and its surroundings.

While many of those businesses have continued to thrive, after World War II the economic and cultural landscape around the ship canal shifted. Suburbs filled Lake Washington's eastern shore. Parks, restaurants, offices, and recreation carved out pieces of the shoreline on both lakes. Today, kayaks, yachts, and excursion boats vie for space on the water with tugs pushing barges and fishing boats coming into port. In sharp contrast to the days when thousands of Seattleites worked in mills, factories, and boatyards on the canal, most people in Seattle now interact with the waterway only when crossing over bridges.

Left: Taken before the cut, this is one of the earliest photographs of the isthmus between Portage Bay and Lake Washington's Union Bay (in the background), now the location of SR 520.

Right: The ship canal and locks define the neighborhoods and industries of Seattle, though not always in the ways their creators envisioned.

THE MCCLELLAN MYTH

Perhaps the most enduring myth associated with the ship canal is a quote attributed to George B. McClellan in which he stated that a canal between Lakes Union and Washington and Puget Sound would "create the finest naval resort in the world." McClellan's support of the canal was often, and is still occasionally, cited as the earliest written statement for the project.

Best known as a general during the Civil War, McClellan was a captain in 1853, when he arrived in Washington Territory as a surveyor for Isaac I. Stevens, recently appointed as territorial governor. Stevens was also in charge of the survey of a potential railroad route from St. Paul, Minnesota, to Puget Sound. McClellan spent most of his time with Stevens east of the Cascades but eventually made it to Puget Sound and Seattle, on January 16, 1854. Shortly thereafter he wrote to Stevens of his exploration: "On the 15th camped on the small lake which connects with the salt water, about five miles north of Seattle. On the 16th reached Seattle; the floating ice gave us much trouble. On the morning of the 17th abandoned the idea of going up the D'Wamish, the ice being so thick and abundant as to close the passage." He concluded that Seattle had an excellent harbor and should be "the proper terminus for any railroad extending to the waters commonly known as Puget sound."

McClellan's supposed endorsement of the canal first appeared in print no later than 1895 but didn't become part of the common mythology until after the 1902 publication of a pro-canal pamphlet by Erastus Brainerd. Brainerd, the main publicist for Seattle during the Klondike Gold Rush, originally published the document to lobby members of Congress in support of the canal. He even cited the specific report—33d Cong. 2d Sess; H.R. Ex. Doc 91—in which McClellan apparently made the point to Secretary of War Jefferson Davis.

Major General George Brinton McClellan, 1862.

The quote and the reference so intrigued Hiram Chittenden that in October 1907 he wrote to the state librarian in Olympia seeking verification. J. M. Hitt wrote back that he could not find "any such reference." Chittenden responded that Brainerd was "rather definite" and that there "must have been some such reference. . . . I do not know exactly how to explain the discrepancy." Ten years later at the dedication of the locks, however, Chittenden concluded, "I very much regret to report that I have been utterly unable to find any confirmation of the McClellan legend to the effect that the prominent man originated the canal idea. I cannot find the slightest evidence . . . that Capt. McClellan ever visited Lake Washington."

Nor has anyone else ever found any evidence of McClellan's quote. Yet it persists, in part because it illustrates a world view held by many early, and some modern, Seattleites: the desire for a stamp of approval from a prominent outsider. If someone such as General McClellan could support the canal, then it must be a good idea and, in turn, Seattle must be a worthy city to receive his blessing.

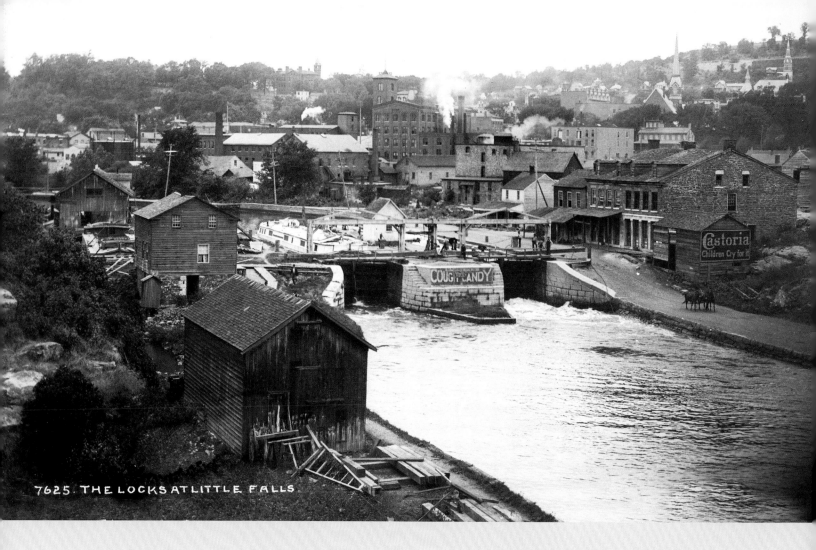

7625. THE LOCKS AT LITTLE FALLS

OTHER CANALS

The first canal proposed in what became the United States was not built until 291 years after Captain Myles Standish suggested it. His plan was to cut a route across Cape Cod, in Massachusetts, in order to create a safer and shorter transportation route from Boston to the south. Standish's canal would not officially open until 1914, which makes the 63 years between Mercer's suggestion and the opening of Seattle's canal seem rather trivial.

Canal building in the United States began in earnest in the 1790s, primarily with short canals that improved navigation along rivers. The first significant one was the Middlesex Canal, which

ran for 27 miles from Boston north to Lowell, Massachusetts. Opened in 1803 at a cost of $500,000, it required 20 locks and eight aqueducts. Although the canal never achieved the financial success that its financers hoped for, it did foster development of factories along the route. Because the Middlesex illustrated that canal transportation was feasible, viable, and efficient, it helped lead to construction of the Erie Canal, which began exactly 100 years before the opening of the Lake Washington Ship Canal.

Opened in October 1825, the 363-mile Erie Canal connected the Hudson River to Lake Erie with 84 masonry locks, each 15 feet wide and 90 feet long. The canal was an immediate financial success, with vast quantities of goods moving east and west along the route. People also traveled on it for pleasure and to move their belongings to new homes. The fare was three to four cents per mile for cargo, which included food, or a penny a mile for emigrants heading westward.

This great success led to what has been called the Canal Era in the United States. Within a decade, more than 2,600 miles of canals snaked across the country, primarily on the eastern seaboard and west to Ohio. All were of similar design, with a waterway, or prism, so named because of the sloped sides of the canal, and a towpath running along the water. Typically four to seven feet deep and less than 70 feet wide, the prism had minimal current. Power came from mules or horses, which walked along the towpath and pulled the narrow canal boats with ropes. Locks were made of wood or masonry or a combination of the two. Most were lift locks, whereby a boat would enter and be either raised or lowered with water.

But the golden era of canals, which lasted up to the Civil War, could not survive the advent of railroads, which were faster, cheaper, and less dependent upon topography. Many canals, abandoned in favor of this new form of transportation, were filled in or left to molder. Those that survived have seen a rebirth. They have become waterways for recreation and nostalgia, and many have been protected as a historical site or park. As Robert J. Kapsch wrote in *Canals*: "Perhaps it is a view of life when travel was leisurely or when technology was understandable: canal remnants of what was state-of-the-art in transportation provide insight into another time, when cargo and passengers were delivered at 4 miles per hour by mild-mannered mules."

Locks on the Erie Canal at Little Falls, New York, circa 1920.

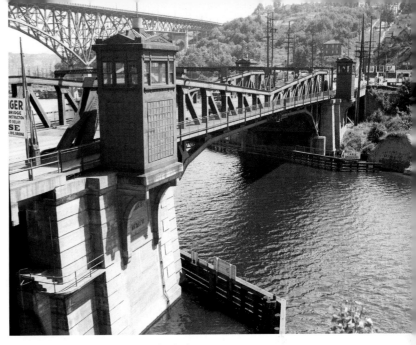

Opened in 1917, the Fremont Bridge is the lowest and busiest span crossing the canal.

The ship canal's environmental and cultural costs have been steep. Lake Washington dropped to the level of Lake Union, creating miles of new land to develop. Salmon Bay changed from a tidal inlet to a freshwater arm of Lake Union and the Black River dried up, which altered the lives of the Native people who had relied on the waterway for more than 10,000 years. In addition, marshlands drained, lakeside vegetation died, and salmon had to find new migration routes.

Like many of Seattle's civil engineering endeavors, it was and is a tradeoff. Thousands of acres of tidelands were buried in Elliott Bay to create an industrial district, lakeshores were filled to build streets, garbage dumps were strategically located to fill ravines and create level land, and the Duwamish was straightened to create a waterway for oceangoing ships. These projects made space for city building, but they also altered or destroyed culturally significant places, displaced people from their homes, disrupted the environment, and damaged habitats. The ship canal could not be built today, but was it an essential piece of infrastructure in the building of the city?

1906 flood on the White River (today's Green River) at Orillia.

At the time it was proposed, the ship canal was envisioned as a solution to a number of problems. First, opening up freshwater harbors in Salmon Bay, Lake Union, and Lake Washington would provide a refuge from wood-boring marine invertebrates. In particular, shipworms preyed upon wooden ships, wooden piers, and rafted logs in salt water and could reduce them to worthless pieces of wood in less than a year. Second, the new harbors would eliminate tidal variations, which had long complicated loading and unloading ships. In addition, from the 1860s until the 1890s, the option of "laying up in ordinary," or storing Navy ships in freshwater during peacetime, was one of the primary reasons the federal government considered building the canal. Puget Sound offered one of the best and most extensive harbors on the West Coast. Save for the Columbia River, which was blocked by a treacherous bar, it was the only one with potential for access to a freshwater harbor.

The canal would also open up about 100 miles of shoreline—much of it level land adjacent to the shore. From the 1850s to the 1910s, most of Elliott Bay abutted steep hillsides. A vast tideflat extended south of King Street and north of about Spokane Street. Access to the Duwamish River valley was limited to shallow-draft vessels, precluding it from being used by oceangoing ships. If Seattle was going to be more than a way station along the Pacific trade routes, it needed room to build wharves, factories, and warehouses.

Classified as a navigation project, the ship canal also had a potential side benefit for flood control on the Duwamish River, which connected with Lake Washington via its outlet, the Black River. On a nearly annual basis the Duwamish would overflow, making it difficult for farms and towns to prosper. The ship canal offered a new outlet for Lake Washington, taking the drainage of more than 1,000 square miles out of the Duwamish River system.

Although the canal offered these advantages and posed limited engineering challenges to construct, it would take more than 60 years to get from Mercer's pronouncement to the opening of the waterway. Over

Right: The locks and ship canal officially opened in July 1917.

Below: This 1920 map, showing the entire planned route of the ship canal, was one of 57 drawings completed by the Army Corps of Engineers.

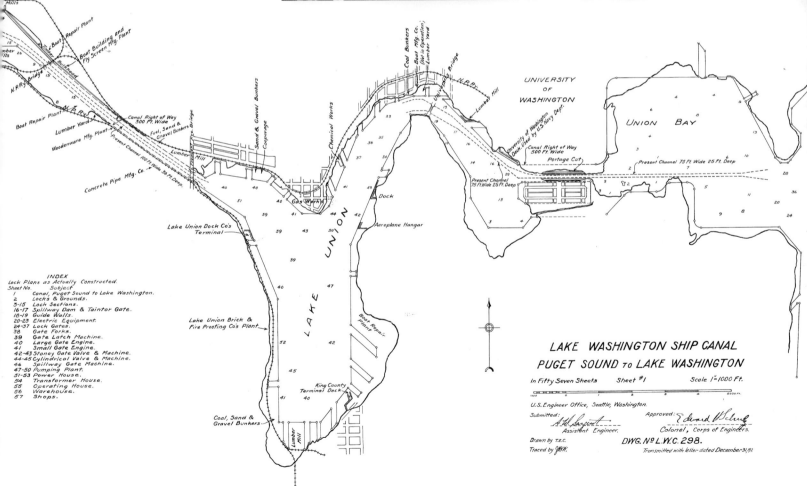

INDEX
Lock Plans as Actually Constructed.
Sheet No.   Subject
1   Canal, Puget Sound to Lake Washington.
2   Locks & Grounds.
3-15   Lock Sections.
16-17   Spillway Dam & Taintor Gate.
18-19   Guide Walls.
20-23   Electric Equipment.
24-37   Lock Gates.
38   Gate Forks.
39   Gate Latch Machine.
40   Large Gate Engine.
41   Small Gate Engine.
42-43   Stoney Gate Valve & Machine.
44-45   Cylindrical Valve & Machine.
46   Spillway Gate Machine.
47-50   Pumping Plant.
51-53   Power House.
54   Transformer House.
55   Operating House.
56   Warehouse.
57   Shops.

LAKE WASHINGTON SHIP CANAL
PUGET SOUND to LAKE WASHINGTON
In Fifty Seven Sheets   Sheet #1   Scale 1"=1000 Ft.

U.S. Engineer Office, Seattle, Washington.
Submitted: Approved: Edward V. Schulz
            Assistant Engineer.   Colonel, Corps of Engineers.
Drawn by T.E.C.   DWG. No L.W.C. 298.
Traced by J.B.W.   Transmitted with letter dated December 31, 192

the decades between 1854 and 1917, there would be numerous Army Corps of Engineers reports, several public meetings, a competing canal proposition to connect Lake Washington with Puget Sound via Elliott Bay, and a variety of schemes to raise the millions of dollars that would be needed to build the locks, cut the canal, pay damages to land- and mill-owners affected by rising waters, and construct drawbridges.

After the canal finally opened officially in 1917, some of the promoters' visions were soon realized. The shoreline of Lake Union and Salmon Bay filled with businesses, and with the United States' involvement in World War I, the city was able to attract investment and government spending. The canal's traffic grew each year and plans were afoot, or at least on the minds of city leaders and Army engineers, to build a third lock. The Great Depression put that idea on hold, as did the outbreak of World War II. By the time the dust had settled from wartime operations, the city was on a different trajectory. Civic leaders had once touted Kirkland's future as the "Pittsburgh of the West," and canal booster and prominent Seattle attorney John J. McGilvra had railed against a proposed park boulevard, writing that "shores will be devoted to trade and commerce, not to fancy boulevards." Instead, when the Lake Washington Floating Bridge opened in 1940, the shoreline quickly filled with homes. Industrial uses did remain at the northern and southern ends of Lake Washington, but they could not compete with people's desire for lakefront homes and suburban subdivisions.

Likewise, not long after the war, a slow shift began along the canal and on Lake Union. Pleasure boats began to rival commercial users of the locks. Moorages for small boats and boat construction and repair companies began to fill more of the piers jutting out from the shore. A 1950 city report discouraged the development of recreational boating facilities on the canal and recommended that the land on the north side of the canal be maintained for industrial uses because the Duwamish River valley did not offer enough land for manufacturers. Just a decade later, the city commissioned another report to explore options for allowing recreation to coexist with industry and to encourage public access to the shore and the waterways. Pleasure boats increasingly used the locks, and commercial boat use continued to decline.

The percentage of shoreline dedicated to industry has dwindled over the past several decades. Condominium and houseboat developments have taken the place of fish-processing and boatbuilding businesses. The Seattle Seahawks football team located

United States Coast Guard lighthouse tender *Hemlock* locking through the large lock, with the Army Corps of Engineers' survey launch *Orcas* in the foreground, circa 1934.

their first training facility at the site of a defunct shipyard and then moved south to the site of a shuttered sawmill near Renton. At Lake Union's south end, the remaining industrial activities, such as the Lake Union Drydock Company, which has been in operation since 1919, sit shoulder to shoulder with restaurants and offices. Nearby is Lake Union Park and the Museum of History and Industry, with Gas Works Park directly north across the lake on an old industrial site. And wrapping around the lake is the Cheshiahud Loop Trail, which offers a route for foot traffic and bicyclists.

Above: Pleasure boats have long outnumbered work boats at the locks.

Left: The locks and ship canal looking east, with downtown and Mount Rainier to the right.

Despite the many changes in the century of the Lake Washington Ship Canal's existence, it has long been one of Seattle's iconic places. Over a million people visit Ballard each year to see the boats lock through between Puget Sound and Salmon Bay. Seattle is the only major U.S. city with a lock connecting salt water and freshwater, which is a central reason for the location of the Puget Sound and North Pacific fishing fleets in Fishermen's Terminal (famous because of the TV show *Deadliest Catch*), the latter of which brings in about half of the entire American seafood catch. Seattle has one of the highest rates of recreational boat ownership in the country, and many of those boats are moored on the lakes, and travel to Puget Sound for fishing or cruising. And the canal still supports industrial development in the city. Businesses that sell boats and provide moorages and services; cement plants that move raw materials; and boatbuilders, tug operators, and drydocks all rely on access to Puget Sound via the locks.

For the past 100 years, Seattle and the Lake Washington Ship Canal and Locks have been intertwined. Not all of the impacts have been positive, and most have been in ways that Thomas Mercer and the early canal supporters could not have imagined. But throughout that century of use, the canal has reflected Seattleites' image of themselves and the city they inhabit and hope to inhabit. Few other places in Seattle are as central to the city's identity.

Detail of Augustus Koch's 1891 "Birds-Eye-View of Seattle and Environs" shows the largely undeveloped shores of Lake Washington.
The trolley on Madison Street (center) leads to a dock at Madison Park, where boats carried people around the lake.

The founding and development of the city [Seattle] have been profoundly influenced by the scour and deposition by Pleistocene continental glaciers together with interglacial and post-glacial alluviation.

– RICHARD W. GALSTER AND WILLIAM T. LAPRADE, "GEOLOGY OF SEATTLE, WASHINGTON, UNITED STATES OF AMERICA," *BULLETIN OF THE ASSOCIATION OF ENGINEERING GEOLOGISTS*

CHAPTER 1

Geology and Native History

Long before we have evidence of people living in the region we now call Seattle, a great sheet of ice spread across the land. Known as the Puget lobe of the Cordilleran Ice Sheet, the 3,000-foot-thick glacier slid out of Canada between the Cascade and Olympic Mountains and passed through this area about 17,400 years ago. The ice continued south, advancing about a mile every three years, to the latitude of Olympia, where it stalled for a few hundred years, then began to retreat, or melt back, to the north. By about 16,400 years ago, the area that would become Seattle was ice-free.

Although the Puget lobe persisted in this region for a relatively short geologic time span, it had a profound influence on the landscape and Seattleites' ability to alter it. Ice and water not only deposited the sediments that are the foundation of the city's terrain, they also shaped the deposits, sculpting them into ridges, valleys, and deep basins. And because this happened so recently, the sediments are relatively soft and the topography relatively easy to manipulate. If older and harder rock made up Seattle's hills, the story of the canal and locks might have been far different.

Deposition of the glacial sediments occurred in several stages. The oldest or lowest layer is the Lawton Clay. (Seven periods of glaciation have occurred in the past two million years; this section describes only the most recent because it had the greatest influence on local topography.) Dark-gray to blue-gray, the Lawton developed in a large lake that filled the Puget lowland from the foothills of the Olympics to the base of the Cascades. The lake formed when the Puget lobe spread south and created a dam across the Strait of Juan de Fuca. As rivers and streams washed out of the glacier, they had nowhere to deposit sediment except in the lake.

In Seattle the Lawton Clay forms a layer up to 100 feet thick, best seen at Discovery Park, formerly known as Fort Lawton. It is the layer of muddy rock directly above the sandstone beds at the base of the bluffs. The reddish-brown sandstone was deposited in the warmer climate that dominated before the last ice age.

Atop the Lawton is the Esperance Sand, a light-gray bed of silt and sand. It also formed through deposition by glacial-derived streams and rivers, not in a lake but on the land in front of the glacier. In Seattle, the Esperance is up to 200 feet thick.

When deposition of the Lawton and Esperance ended, which corresponded with the Puget lobe advancing through Seattle, several hundred feet of sediment filled the lowlands. Punctuated by only a handful of landforms, including Green and Gold Mountains on the Kitsap Peninsula and Newcastle Hills, Tiger Mountain, and Cougar Mountain, the clay, silt, and sand formed a gently rolling plain that sloped and thinned to the south. (You can still see the high point of the plain; around Seattle it's equal in elevation (about 450 feet) to the tops of the hills here and out on the islands such as Bainbridge and Vashon.)

The final period of deposition during the advance of the Puget lobe occurred as the ice ground across the plain and deposited a thin sheet of sand, cobbles, gravel, and boulders atop the great plain. City residents know this final layer of glacial sediment as hardpan, a very resistant material only a few to 10 feet thick, though it can reach a depth of 30 feet. Geologists call it the Vashon till.

The 3,000-foot-thick Puget lobe extended to about Olympia before melting or retreating back to Canada.

Right: Typical vegetation along the shore of Lake Washington, 1895.

As the glacier moved south it also began to sculpt the land. Shaping occurred in two manners: deep incision by water and shaving by ice. The water-carved incisions—Duwamish River valley, Lake Sammamish, Lake Washington, and Puget Sound—formed as rivers flowing under the ice cut troughs down into the poorly consolidated layers of glacial sediment. Geologists have estimated that the rivers carried away more than 180 cubic miles of material, or enough to cover all of Seattle in two feet of sediment.

The role of the ice was less dramatic but equally as noticeable. As the glacier moved south, it acted like a giant rake and formed a series of more or less parallel hills and valleys, such as Queen Anne and Interbay. These structures run primarily in a north-south orientation, the direction of movement of the glacier, except for one notable feature. The long cut across the landscape where the ship canal is located bucks the regional topography and instead runs northwest to southeast. Water flowing at the base of the ice most likely carved the waterway. The glacier also appears to have stalled at this point on its retreat, which would have provided additional water for erosion. The bigger question is why a topographic low cuts against the grain. Either a structure buried deep in the bedrock or a tectonic break could have influenced erosion, but geologists have yet to find conclusive evidence for this anomaly.

With the retreat of the ice, another dramatic change in the land occurred. It slowly began to rise, or rebound, as the great weight of the ice melted away. Simultaneously, sea level began to rise as the water formerly locked up in the continent-covering ice sheets began to flow off the land and into the ocean. As happened when the Puget lobe first arrived, water from the melting glacier began to fill the subglacial, river-carved troughs and formed a multi-fingered body of water that eventually covered most of the Puget lowland and connected Puget Sound to Lake Washington.

This large freshwater lake persisted for a little over a thousand years, until the combination of sea-level rise and glacial retreat allowed salt water to flow into Puget Sound and the surrounding lowlands. For the next 700 years Lake Washington was as salty as the sea. Eventually, the land's rebound exceeded the rise of sea level and severed the lake's connection to salt water, and Lake Washington has been a freshwater lake for the past 14,800 years.

Once that basic differentiation between salt- and freshwater basins was established, area waterbodies began developing into the waterways that would inspire the canal's conception.

Lake Washington Boulevard near Seward Park, June 1913.

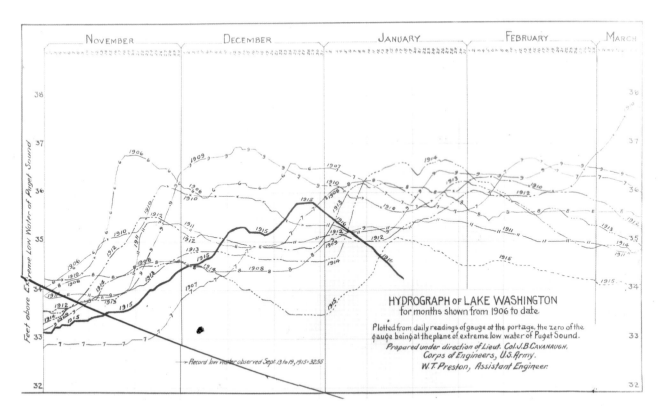

HYDROGRAPH of LAKE WASHINGTON
for months shown from 1906 to date

Plotted from daily readings of gauge at the portage, the zero of the
gauge being at the plane of extreme low water of Puget Sound.
Prepared under direction of Lieut. Col.J.B.Cavanaugh,
Corps of Engineers, U.S.Army.
W.T.Preston, Assistant Engineer.

Feet above Extreme Low Water of Puget Sound

Record low water observed Sept. 13 to 19, 1915 = 32.55

This hydrographic chart created by the Army Corps of Engineers shows the elevation difference between
Lake Washington and the extreme low tide of Puget Sound between 1906 and 1916.

Lake Washington

Originally located about 29 feet above sea level, Lake Washington is the state's second-largest natural lake: 22 miles long with an average width of 1.5 miles. Because of the subglacial scouring, Lake Washington is deep, averaging 108 feet to the muddy bottom, with a maximum depth of 214 feet just north of the Interstate 90 floating bridge and west of Mercer Island. The lake originally had 82 miles of shoreline and almost 1,100 acres of wetlands. These bogs and marshes provided critical habitat for fish, birds, mammals, and emergent vegetation, all of which were important resources for the Native people who lived around the lake. By about 7,000 years ago, a classic northwest forest of Douglas fir, western red cedar, and western hemlock and dense understory covered the landscape.

Water entered the lake primarily through the Sammamish River, in its northeast corner. Additional sources included numerous springs and seeps, as well as at least 19 named creeks (Coal, Fairweather, Forbes, Frink, Juanita, Kelsey, Lyon, Madrona, Mapes, May, McAleer, Mt. Baker, Ravenna, Taylor, Thornton, Washington Park, Wetmore, Yarrow, and Yesler). Depending on rainfall and snowmelt, the surface elevation of Lake Washington ranged about seven feet, with the highest level typically in late winter/early spring. Water drained via the Black River at the lake's south end.

Downstream Pathways

BLACK RIVER – THE OUTLET

Sinuous and shallow (about 4 feet deep), the Black River originally flowed for three miles from Lake Washington to a confluence with the White River, which also included water from the Green River. Before 1906, the Green entered the White near Auburn, but a damaging flood that year had, with some help from King County residents, turned the waters of the White River into the Stuck River channel. Because the Stuck flowed toward Tacoma, the White no longer had a confluence with the Green. Therefore, after 1906, the Black flowed into the Green, and the united waterways continued as the Duwamish River. The colorful names came about because in contrast to the light-colored Green and White, the Black carried dark sediment that washed out of the Cedar River.

For most of the year, the Black flowed quietly, but when Lake Washington was high, the river ripped along in floods that could result in large sections of the Duwamish valley being underwater for weeks at a time. Flooding in the Black also occurred when the Cedar ran high, which could lead to an unusual situation whereby the Cedar had enough water to reverse the upper flow of the Black and push it into Lake Washington. This is the origin of the Chinook Jargon—a regional trade language—name for the Black, Mox La Push, or "two mouths." Flooding downstream was exacerbated because the lake acted as a giant holding tank and slowly released the water, which prolonged the high water.

Black River around 1911, possibly the Hayes Farm, near the present-day location of the Renton Airport Control Tower.

DUWAMISH RIVER – THE CONNECTION TO ELLIOTT BAY

The Duwamish is a relatively young river. At the end of the last ice age, instead of the broad valley that now exists, a deep trough, or arm, of Puget Sound extended 20 miles south to about modern-day Auburn. The trough was not long-lived, at least from a geologic point of view. Around 5,600 years ago, Mount Rainier erupted and generated a massive mudflow known as the Osceola lahar, which cascaded down the mountain and deposited 4.9 billion cubic yards of debris onto the land and into the troughs of the Puget lowland. Over the next several thousand years, three subsequent mudflows carried enough sediment to fill in the trough and form the Duwamish River valley. When the last of these lahars hit about 1,100 years ago, it pushed the mouth of the river to its present-day location in Elliott Bay.

That mouth, or delta, was a broad tideflat of mud that stretched from the base of Beacon Hill to the base of the West Seattle peninsula. It extended more than three quarters of a mile south of the modern-day West Seattle Bridge and Spokane Street viaduct. At high tide, a sheet of water 10 to 15 feet deep completely covered the delta. At low tide, the mud was an open expanse incised by numerous rivulets. Upstream, the Duwamish meandered through forests of western red cedar, Douglas fir, black cottonwood, red alder, Oregon ash, and bigleaf maple. Some of the trees were up to eight feet in diameter and many leaned into the river, making navigation challenging. From its confluence with the Black, the Duwamish twisted for 14 miles to reach Elliott Bay, though the straight-line distance from that point is a little over seven miles.

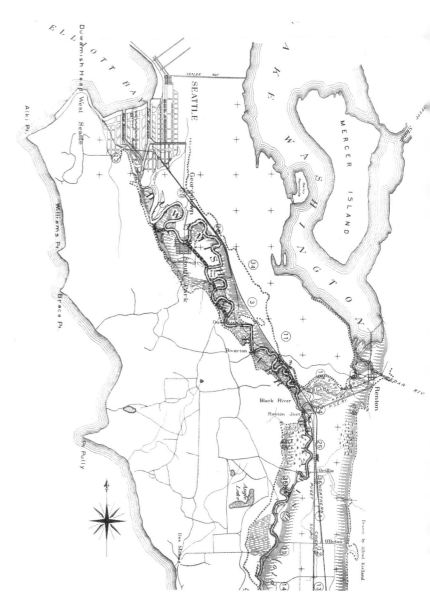

Originally a sinuous river that wound its way across a broad, flat valley, the Duwamish (shown here in 1907) began to be dredged and straightened in 1913.

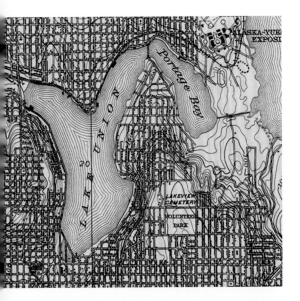

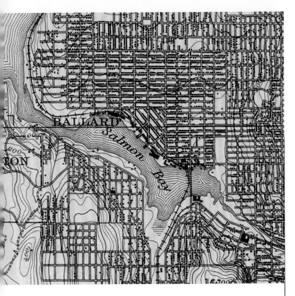

Details of Lake Union and Salmon Bay from 1909 United States Geological Survey map of Seattle.

LAKE UNION – THE LINK

Located about 20 feet above sea level, Lake Union is a kettle lake, meaning it formed from a melting chunk of ice that remained after the last glaciation. Its main subsequent water supply was from springs, runoff, and creeks, which led to a minimal lake-level fluctuation of one to three feet. Early maps show that the southwest corner of the lake extended to the south of modern-day Mercer Street and west almost to modern-day Eighth Avenue North, nearly 600 feet from the modern shoreline. The lake was also wider on its southeast margin, spreading almost to Eastlake Avenue between East Howe and East Galer.

Most of the main body of the lake is between 35 and 40 feet deep; the Portage Bay arm was about half that deep. Lake Union drained out its northwest corner via Ross Creek, which was narrow enough that a surveyor in 1855 was able to step across it. Lake Union was separated from Lake Washington by a low ridge of land—the Montlake Portage—less than a half mile wide.

SALMON BAY – THE SALTWATER CONNECTION

Connected to Puget Sound via a narrow passage, Salmon Bay was a tidal saltwater inlet where the water level fluctuated on average about 11 feet between high and low tides. At low tide, little water remained and the bay was mostly mud, with a narrow channel just three feet deep extending out to Puget Sound. At the highest tides, the water extended into Interbay, between Queen Anne and Magnolia, to about modern-day Ruffner Street, a quarter mile south of its present extent. To the east, the water would have spread almost to modern-day Eighth Avenue West, a little more than one-half mile up the modern Fremont Cut from the Ballard Bridge.

The Upstream Sources

LAKE SAMMAMISH AND SAMMAMISH RIVER

Historically known as Squak Slough and Squak Lake (the name is derived from the Lushootseed name for the area at the southern end of the lake), the Sammamish River and Lake Sammamish watershed was the primary source of water to Lake Washington. Flowing for

South side of Salmon Bay

about 17 miles, although only 12 miles separated the lakes, the river meandered extensively with oxbow lakes (abandoned river bends) and widespread wetlands. Historic reports note that when the river flooded, which occurred regularly, and it was foggy, riverboats would have to stop because the captains could not distinguish the main river channel from the many flooded side channels.

It is unclear how much elevation separated Lake Washington and Lake Sammamish. Reports vary from 4 feet to 9.6 feet, with the larger number in an 1891 Army Corps of Engineers report. All accounts, however, agree that river flow between the lakes was extremely slow (the *Seattle Post-Intelligencer* once described the river as "pursuing its slothful way"), which may account for the use of *slough* in the river's historic name of Squak Slough. An 1897 Land Classification map from the U.S. Geological Survey showed the floodplain/river valley as a wetland. The river was navigable though and shallow-draft steamers regularly traveled the waterway towing log rafts and carrying passengers and goods, such as coal, albeit not at a speedy pace.

CEDAR RIVER

Beginning at Twilight Lake (elevation 3,575 feet), about five miles southwest of Snoqualmie Pass, the Cedar River came out of the Cascade Mountains and flowed for 55 miles *almost* to Lake Washington at its south end near Renton. It then turned and joined the Black River. Although the Cedar did not enter Lake Washington, it played a critical role in the lake's surface elevation. As the water ran out of the steep mountains and met the relatively flat lowlands, it slowed down and dropped the debris it carried. Typically this was sand and gravel, but during flood stage the Cedar could transport logs, boulders, and other substantial sediment, all of which contributed to forming what geologists call an alluvial fan.

Over the centuries and millennia, as the fan grew with continued deposition from the Cedar, it acted as a dam, blocking the outlet of the lake. Because of the dam, the lake rose incrementally behind it, though it was never completely blocked for long. Water always cut an escape route through the alluvial material and found a path out through the Black River. But then the cycle would begin again: more sediment, higher dam, higher lake level, and escape.

Geologists can trace a rise in the lake level of almost 70 feet over the past 14,500 years, leaving Lake Washington at its historic elevation of 29 feet above sea level before construction of the ship canal.

Alfred Schillestad was 20 years old when he made this sketch in 1889. His parents, Ole and Regina, built a home on Salmon Bay across from the present location of the locks; it had to be moved when the water in the bay was raised following the completion of the locks.

NATIVE VILLAGES AND HISTORIC AND MODERN TOWNS

1   páq̓áčałču ("Brush Spread on the Water")
2   šilšul ("Tucked Away Inside")
3   Ballard
4   Ross
5   Fremont
6   Edgewater
7   Latona
8   sluʔwił ("Little Canoe Channel")
9   Yesler
10   Pontiac
11   dxWXóóbud ("Silenced (Quieted) Place")
12   ƛ̓aX̌ʷadis ("something planted erect by a house fire")
13   Kirkland/Houghton
14   Medina
15   sáʔcaqał ("Water at Head of the Bay")/ Mercer Slough
16   Mercer Island
17   Newcastle
18   dəwabqwuʔ ("Confluence")
19   Renton
20   Columbia City
21   Leschi
22   Madison Park

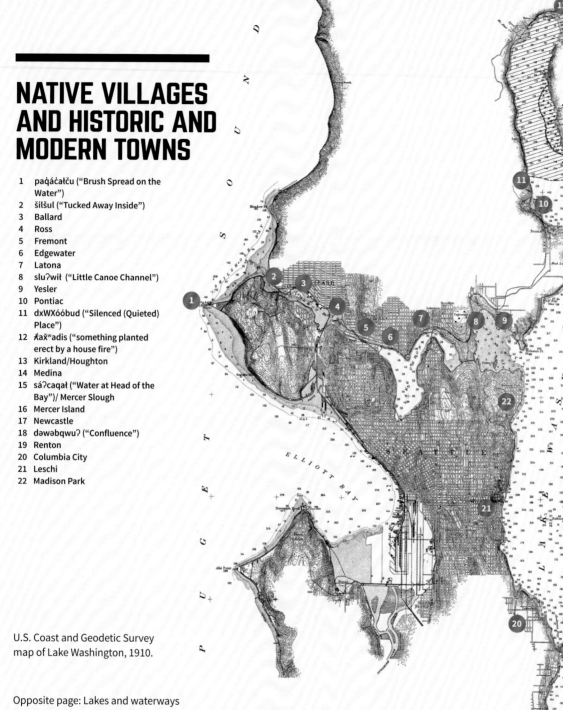

U.S. Coast and Geodetic Survey map of Lake Washington, 1910.

Opposite page: Lakes and waterways have long influenced the development of Seattle and its neighborhoods. In this 1962 image the neighborhood of Montlake is contained by the cut and soon to be split by the new SR 520 bridge. The former town of Yesler was located at the edge of the swamp in Union Bay at the top of the image.

TOWNS

TOWNS Throughout the early history of Seattle many developers attempted to start their own towns on its outskirts, particularly around Lake Washington. Some thrived, such as Ballard, which had 17,000 people in 1907, but most remained quite small, with a few shops, perhaps some industry, and maybe even a post office. Most of the towns were either annexed and became neighborhoods or simply disappeared off maps. Seattle subsumed Fremont, Edgewater, and Latona in 1891, Ballard in 1907, and Yesler in 1910.

Ballard – Incorporated in 1890 on land partially owned by William Rankin Ballard, Ballard was one of the larger towns in King County when Seattle annexed it.

Fremont – Edward C. Kilbourne, Edward and Carrie Blewett, and Luther H. Griffith named Fremont in 1888 for the Nebraska hometown of Griffith and the Blewetts.

Ross – Never established as a formal town, Ross was more a collection of houses, a post office, and a school on land that John Ross filed a claim for in 1853.

Edgewater – Corliss P. Stone established Edgewater in 1889 and named it for a Chicago lakeside community.

Latona – Developed by James Moore in 1889, Latona consisted of 350 lots and was reached by the Seattle, Lake Shore and Eastern Railway Company and a steamer that plied Lake Union.

Yesler – Henry Yesler platted his company town in 1888 to house employees of a sawmill he built on the lake.

Pontiac – Home to a brick factory and shipbuilding facility, Pontiac was large enough to merit a post office in 1890. Although no one can claim to have established Pontiac, early settler Osborn Merritt came from Pontiac, Michigan. By 1914, no industry and few people remained

Native Communities

Thomas Mercer may have been the first settler to mention Lake Union as a link between salt water and freshwater, but people have been using these corridors between the interior lakes and salt water for thousands of years. The earliest evidence of humans in the region comes from a site along Bear Creek in Redmond, about 1.5 miles north of Lake Sammamish and just east of the Sammamish River. Using pieces of willow found there, archaeologists have radiocarbon dated it to about 12,000 years ago, making it the oldest archaeological site in western Washington. The site, which is on a slight rise above a wetland, appears to have been a camp where people gathered to hunt and fish and make stone tools.

Archaeologists excavated more than 4,000 stone artifacts at Bear Creek, including flakes, scrapers, projectile points, and hammerstones. They were made from basalt, quartzite, and chert, all locally available rock. Residue on the stone artifacts indicates that whoever made the tools used the items to hunt large game such as bear, deer, and bighorn sheep, as well as to catch salmon.

Other sites in the Lake Washington region show that people have lived in this area more or less continuously since the time of those who lived at the Bear Creek site. These include locations along the Sammamish River, at Marymoor Park, on the north side of Salmon Bay, and on the Magnolia peninsula at West Point. Based on the thousands of artifacts, which range from simple beads to razor-sharp knife blades to elaborately carved animal representations, archaeologists have proposed that the ancient inhabitants moved seasonally across the landscape, hunting and gathering the abundant plant and animal resources on the land and in the water.

Although archaeologists do not have specific evidence of how these people traveled, it is reasonable to think that they would have used waterways to avoid the forests and hills that made overland travel challenging. If this is the case, it is likely that they floated down or walked along the Sammamish River to Lake Washington and continued out to Puget Sound via Lake Union and Salmon Bay, thus starting the long tradition of using this route as a central means of linking freshwater and salt water.

In addition, archaeological evidence illustrates that people have also moved between Lake Washington and Puget Sound via the Duwamish and Black Rivers. Of the many sites excavated on those waterways, dating from about 2,000 years ago to the time of European settlement, one of the more thoroughly studied is known as Tualdad Altu, or King Salmon's House. Located along the Black River and dated at 1,700 years old, Tualdad Altu consisted of a midden and a longhouse at least 55 feet in length. Artifacts included bone harpoon points, awls, and matting needles, stone blades, scrapers, and whetstones, and stone and bone ornaments. The inhabitants took full advantage of the wide diversity of animals that lived here. Within the sites are remains as diverse as beaver, bufflehead, and many types of shellfish, though salmon was the most important food.

In more recent times, Lake Washington continued to be a central resource for Native people across the region. Closest to the lake, the Duwamish reached it by trail or by boat. East of the lake were the Snoqualmie, who traveled down from Lake Sammamish, and to the west were the Suquamish, who came over from their winter villages on the Kitsap Peninsula. Dennis Lewarch, Tribal Historic Preservation Officer for the Suquamish tribe, notes

Collected at the Bear Creek site in Redmond, this stone projectile point was dated between 10,000 and 12,500 years old.

Below: Coast Salish family in cedar canoe, circa 1912.

that because the Suquamish did not have a large body of freshwater on the peninsula, they paddled across Puget Sound to exploit the lake's resources. "For people whose central means of transportation was the canoe, traveling between the different bodies of water would not have seemed challenging," said Lewarch. They were used to portaging, or carrying their canoes, much greater distances. Or they could have simply left canoes where needed and had only to carry their gear from bay to lake, load the awaiting canoe, and continue moving on water.

Those who came to the lake would have harvested plants such as tule, cattails, and wapato, as well as fur-bearing animals, including muskrat and otter. Another important food staple was kokanee, non-migratory salmon that spend their entire lives in freshwater. Generally smaller than their oceangoing relatives, sockeye, kokanee were the most prized salmon in the region, according to historian David Buerge, who has extensively researched the Duwamish Tribe's history.

Historic records show seven winter village sites situated around Lake Washington. Each village clustered around a stream where salmon spawned. Within those villages there were at least 18 longhouse sites. Most longhouses were about 50 feet wide by 100 feet long, though a few measured 60 by 120 feet. They took months to build and incorporated big cedar logs for framing and split cedar for siding. Inside were platforms for beds, fireplaces for each of the several families that resided within, and lofts for storing food and provisions. Lining the walls was matting, often with elaborate woven designs.

Around each village were several acres of cleared land, which some residents could have used for small-scale farming. The people also burned the underbrush to create good hunting grounds and areas to harvest berries. But the lake was the main source of food.

Top to bottom: Jadeite adze blade in wood, basalt chopper/scraper, and antler awl collected at the locks site in 1923-1924. The awl is about 8.5 inches long.

Men built weirs near the mouths of the streams. They harvested the fish with dip nets, stabbed them with double-pronged spears, or gathered them in great seine nets. Hunters also used nets to capture the many migratory birds that visited the lake for stopovers.

Buerge estimates that perhaps 700 or so people lived around Lake Washington at any one time, with four or five families in each house. The people were known generally as Hah-chu-ahbsh, the "lake people," though Buerge points out that ethnographer Thomas Waterman recorded several subgroups in the 1910s. The Salmon Bay people were known as Sheel-shol-ahbsh; *sheel-shol* has been translated as "tucked away inside." Those living around Lake Union were Ha-ah-chu-ahbsh, "littlest lake people," and those on Lake Sammamish were Haht-hah-chu-ahbsh, "second lake people." "The meanings of these names indicated that all three lakes were conceived to be related," said Buerge.

He believes that the Native people had a hydrographic sense of the landscape, where Shilshole was the foot and Issaquah Creek, at the upper end of Lake Sammamish, was the head. The inhabitants and the place were interconnected and interdependent. The people found sustenance. They constructed homes. They built lives centered on this unique corridor linking salt water and freshwater. "The modern canal," said Buerge, "is simply the industrial iteration of what the Native people were doing for thousands of years."

Hwelchteed, known to most early settlers as Salmon Bay Charlie, was a Sheel-shol-ahbsh. He and his wife Cheethluleetsa, or Madeline, owned 10 acres on the bay.

A Bird's Eye View of Lake Union, Union Bay and
Lake Washington, showing the Lake Washington Canal
as it will look upon completion.

SEATTLE
U.S.A.

Photo by F

A survey was made last week for a canal to connect Lake Washington and Lake Union… The project is an important one, as it would open the greater part of the distance from the Bay to the coal mines back of Lake Washington to water transportation; and, also, draw off a portion of the water that would flow down Black River, thus preventing that and Dwamish valleys from inundation during freshets.

– PUGET SOUND WEEKLY,
DECEMBER 24, 1866

CHAPTER 2

Early History: 1854-1892

On July 4, 1854, the citizens of the recently established village of Seattle gathered on the shore of a small lake known in the local Chinook Jargon as *tenas chuck*, or "little waters." The party of Seattleites had walked or ridden horses for about two miles north to reach the lake from their small community of homes on Elliott Bay. After climbing over a low hill, they would have dropped down to their destination, property homesteaded by their fellow settlers Thomas Mercer and David and Louisa Denny.

We know little about the gathering except that Mercer made a prophetic speech to his assembled friends and family. First, he proposed bestowing the name Washington on what was then known by a variety of names: Lake Geneva, Lake Duwamish, or *hyas chuck*, Chinook Jargon for "big waters." Mercer then suggested the name Union for the smaller lake where everyone had gathered, noting the possibility "of this little body of water sometime providing a connecting link uniting the larger lake and Puget Sound." Several weeks later, at a more formal gathering, the little town's citizens officially voted to bestow the new names: Lake Union and Lake Washington.

At the time, Mercer's dream of uniting fresh and salt water must have seemed just that, a dream that was hardly possible. The 22 members of Seattle's founding families had arrived only two and a half years earlier. Now grown to perhaps 100 to 150 people, Seattle was still a tiny enclave, barely carved out of a nearly impenetrable forest of some of the largest trees on Earth. About a mile of land and another mile of tidal inlet separated Lake Union from Puget Sound. The two lakes were closer but still divided by a 2,000-foot-wide headland, which rose more than 35 feet above the water.

It is not clear why Mercer made his proposal. A former woolen mill worker and farmer from the Midwest, he did not come to Seattle with a background in either engineering or a field that traditionally relied on water travel. He could have been inspired by the Erie Canal, which was nationally known and had been completed when Mercer was a boy, but we have no explicit evidence for this connection. Most likely it was his unusual circumstances in Seattle that led to his statement. Mercer was a hauler of goods, using his horse and wagon to travel Seattle's primitive trails. He was also the earliest settler to live on Lake Union. These two facets of his life would have enabled him to explore the shoreline and realize the importance of the location as a good travel corridor. In addition, Mercer was well acquainted with the Native people and could have been inspired after seeing them canoeing along the route between salt water and freshwater and witnessing their portages.

But there is also a bit of a mystical side to Mercer. In his 1891 *History of Seattle*, Frederic James Grant wrote that Mercer had a dream in which he appeared to be in a "forest where there was a sidehill swamp with a lake beyond and a bay upon which one might come to his home all the way in a boat." No matter why Mercer offered up his vision, his son-in-law, historian Clarence Bagley, wrote that Mercer "was exceedingly anxious to see the Lake Washington canal completed." Although he died in May 1898 and didn't see the final canal, Thomas Mercer did at least live long enough to see an initial connection made.

Looking east across Portage Bay, the Montlake neighborhood, and the Montlake log canal toward Laurelhurst, which was just beginning to be developed, circa 1900.

Nineteen-year-old Harvey L. Pike was the first to take up Mercer's idea. Pike had come to Seattle with his parents (Pike Street honors his father) and worked as a painter. In June 1861, he bartered $242.75 of manual labor clearing land for 161.83 acres between the two lakes. He probably knew of the parcel because he worked on the University of Washington, which, although still located downtown, owned the rural land to the north of the settlement. This property had been set aside by the United States Congress in 1854 for a territorial university, and the university was selling a portion of it to generate money for the nascent school.

Sometime after acquiring his land, Pike began to cut a channel using a pick, shovel, and wheelbarrow. It seems doubtful that he could have made much progress in this way. Or did he? One account states that Pike connected the lakes with a narrow ditch just wide enough for water to trickle through (when the lake level was high from winter rains), but that document was not written until 1903. No other account describes Pike's work as anything more than an attempt.

PLAN OF UNION CITY

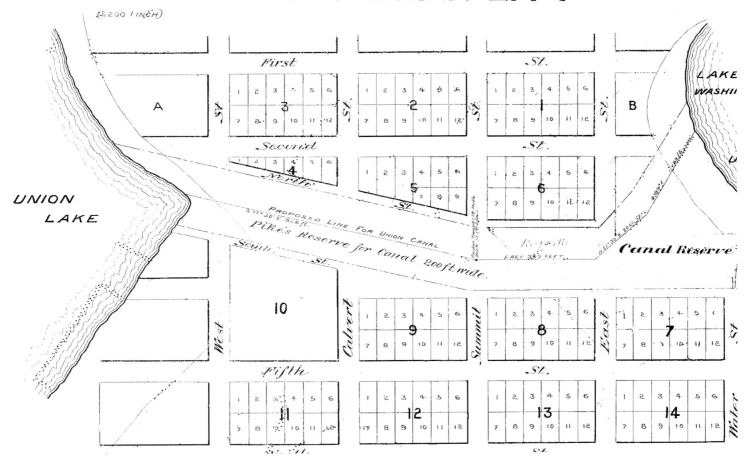

Harvey Pike's plat of Union City, 1869.

Unfortunately, few contemporary documents exist from the early history of the canal. One that does survive provides insight into the long-term motivations for canal construction. It is a memorial, or formal request, written by the Territorial Legislature to the United States Congress; memorials such as this one had no legal authority but expressed the concerns of local citizens. Crafted in January 1868, the memorial addressed flooding in the Duwamish River valley and surrounding lands. The memorialists would "ever pray" that "by connecting lakes Union and Washington by a canal, these lands would be reclaimed and great relief afforded to the settlers."

No matter how much of a ditch Pike excavated, he did have ambitious ideas. On June 24, 1869, he filed the Plan of Union City on land now crossed by the modern State Route 520. Between Lake Washington and Lake Union, Pike reserved space for a 200-foot-wide canal, which bent to the north in order to connect the closest shorelines. (One of the unknowns about Pike is when exactly did he work on his ditch. Logically it was sometime between the time he acquired the land in 1861 and when he platted it in 1869, but we have no unequivocal evidence of a specific date.) Pike's Union City also included 147 lots, the first of which he sold to his mother for $50. Over the next two years, he laid out

COAL AND THE CANAL

In 1853, homesteader Reuben Bigelow was the first white settler to discover coal in the area when he accidentally uncovered a bed of it near his land on the Black River. Other discoveries followed, all on the east side of Lake Washington, and in 1868 geologist T. A. Blake reported that "it will not be easy to over-estimate the future importance of the Seattle coal field to the commercial and productive interests of the Pacific Coast." There was one significant problem: without a railroad or good roads, there was no easy method for transporting the coal.

This challenge was well known; four years before Blake's report, the *Seattle Gazette* had praised William Perkins because he had taken the initiative to build a boat to bring coal from mines at Squak Lake (now Lake Sammamish) to Elliott Bay, but it had taken nearly three weeks to complete the journey. Two weeks after Perkins' trip, the March 1, 1864, *Gazette* suggested a "better and far shorter route." The unnamed author proposed cutting a canal about 300 yards long between Union Bay and Lake Union. "The water in Washington Lake is said to be several feet higher than in Lake Union and it is contended that a mere ditch through which to turn the water is all that is required, and the canal will *make itself*." This appears to be the earliest mention in print of such a canal and may also have prompted Harvey Pike's quixotic canal attempt.

Motivated to find a cheap way to transport coal, a group of investors decided to build Seattle's first railroad. Opened on March 22, 1872, and operated by the Seattle Coal & Transportation Company, the little train ran from the south end of Lake Union to about Front Street (now First Avenue) and Pike Street. In order for the coal to reach the railroad, it started in a mine at Newcastle then traveled by tram to Lake Washington, where it was placed on a scow that carried it to the west end of Union Bay. The cars of coal were then transported by tram across the Portage at Montlake to a barge that took the coal to the railroad. By the end of its travels, the coal had been handled 11 times.

Although more efficient than previous routes, the SC&T railroad did not allow Seattle to live up to Blake's expectations. Finally, in

Top: First map to show a canal route linking Lake Washington and Lake Union, from *Seattle Gazette*, March 1, 1864.

Bottom: When the Seattle Coal & Transportation Company began operating in 1872, Seattle celebrated with what the *Seattle P-I* described as "unanimity never before equaled on any occasion in the city."

1877, a new railroad from Elliott Bay to Renton, operated by the Seattle and Walla Walla Railroad and Transportation Company, eliminated the lake-to-lake route and helped make Seattle the most important supplier of coal on the Pacific coast.

Coal and a canal also had a role in the gubernatorial election of 1892. Four years earlier, an English steel manufacturer, Peter Kirk, had announced that he would build a steel plant on the east side of Lake Washington, at what is now Kirkland. Nearby were the raw ingredients he needed: iron and limestone (for smelting) near Snoqualmie Pass and coal from Newcastle. Kirk's initial plan was to transport the steel via the Seattle, Lake Shore and Eastern Railway (now the route of the Burke-Gilman Trail), which ran along the north shore of Lake Washington, but ideally he wanted to ship it out via a canal that connected Lake Washington with Puget Sound.

Over the next few years, Kirk's company, Moss Bay Iron and Steel Works, built machine, blacksmith, and pattern shops and a foundry building. Kirk and his fellow investors also began lobbying for their canal, which they claimed would bring abundant jobs and help make Kirkland the "Pittsburgh of the West." But detractors labeled it the Seattle, or Kirkland, Ditch and claimed that it would benefit only the Kirkland syndicate and others in Seattle. The anti-canal sentiment continued to simmer until the 1892 election, when most people outside Seattle decried the ditch. As is still the case today, however, Seattle was much more populous than the rest of the state, and the city's voters rallied behind and elected the pro-canal candidate. But the infighting within the state led to the federal government not providing any funding, and within a year, Kirk's steel mill dream was over, never to surface again.

Moss Bay Iron and Steel Works, circa 1892.

Detail of Eli S. Glover's "Bird's Eye View of the City of Seattle," 1878. Smoke from the Seattle Coal & Transportation Company train (center) can be seen as it carries coal from Lake Union to the coal bunker on a large pier on the waterfront at Pike Street (left). This was one of the proposed routes for a northern canal.

additions to the north and south of Union City and continued to sell pieces of property.

He also helped form the Lake Washington Canal Company on January 6, 1871, which had the goal of building a canal and locks from Puget Sound to Lake Washington "and to navigate the same with steamers or other water crafts." His fellow investors were James McNaught, a well-connected Seattle lawyer and entrepreneur; James R. Robbins, a Seattle businessman; and two men from the area around The Dalles, Oregon, John H. Fairchild and Orlando Humason. Although the company made no progress and soon disbanded, Pike did sell three pieces of property to the LWCC and Robbins and McNaught for $1,100.

Likely unbeknownst to Pike, the federal government was also interested in a canal connecting Puget Sound to Lake Washington. In 1867, Brigadier General Barton S. Alexander, senior military engineer for the Army Corps of Engineers on the Pacific coast, had organized a survey for military defense of the coast. Part of that survey involved an exploration of Puget Sound as a possible site for a naval port. Alexander concluded that Lake Washington had the potential to be a port but would require a canal to connect it to Puget Sound. Three years later, Alexander formally asked the Corps' Board of Engineers for Fortifications in San Francisco for money to survey the lake, which he wrote would "furnish us with an admirable position for a naval depot with almost every requirement which could be desired."

In December 1871, Alexander released his survey, which had been completed by engineer Lieutenant Thomas H. Handbury. Handbury favored the shortest route possible by connecting Lake Union directly to Elliott Bay. Known as Mercer's Farm route, it extended in a straight line for a little less than a mile from the southwest corner of Lake Union, which at the time was at about modern-day Mercer Street, to the bay near Battery Street. Handbury's second route followed the path of the Seattle Coal & Transportation Company's tramway, which ran from a coal bunker at the base of Pike Street east to about modern-day Westlake Avenue and then turned north down a valley to the southeast corner of the lake. This line traversed lower ground than the farm route but was more than 1,000 feet longer. Total cost for each would be $4.7 million, or between $615 million and $1.24 billion in current dollars.

Despite the challenge of having to make a 119-foot-deep cut for his preferred Mercer's Farm route, Alexander prioritized it over a canal connecting Lake Union and Shilshole Bay because a canal at that location required too much dredging and would suffer from exposure to the "cannonade of an enemy in time of war." He also eliminated a line that followed the Black River and Duwamish River to Elliott Bay because it was too long and terminated in a shallow estuary. Alexander concluded that although the Puget Sound region offered one of only three places on the Pacific coast to build a secure port for the United States Navy, the area possessed too few people and resources to justify further study.

Alexander's assessment aside, Seattle had grown significantly since Mercer's speech. More than 1,100 people now lived on the slopes rising from Elliott Bay. Seattle was becoming one of the centers of trade on Puget Sound, with a half dozen wharves lining the shoreline, the early development of a coal industry, and a growing collection of small businesses, including sash and door factories, gristmills, and cigar manufacturers. In the words

of one newspaper writer, "Seattle has sloughed off a great deal of its provincialism, and, more than any other place I have seen, seems to be getting ready for a metropolitan career."

Another decade would pass, however, before serious consideration of a canal resurfaced. Again it was up to Seattleites to take charge. In early March 1883, a group of investors led by Thomas Burke, David Denny, Guy Phinney, and Benjamin F. Day formed the Lake Washington Improvement Company. All of the men owned land around Lake Union, which was starting to become a manufacturing center with a sawmill (soon to be owned by Denny) at the south end of the lake and two nearby brick factories capable of producing 750,000 bricks per year.

The Improvement Company's first task was to hire the firm of Scurry and Snow to survey potential canal routes

Yesler's Wharf was one of the largest on the Seattle waterfront in 1878.

ARMY CORPS OF ENGINEERS

Thomas Jefferson created the Corps of Engineers in 1802 with operations based at the United States Military Academy in West Point, New York. The goal was to provide engineers for public works such as forts, roads, aqueducts, and lighthouses. In 1824, the Supreme Court ruled in *Gibbons v. Ogden* that the federal government's authority extended over riverine navigation under the Commerce Clause of the Constitution. Congress first authorized surveys of road and navigation routes for commercial, military, or mail-delivery purposes, which President John Quincy Adams assigned to the Corps. Congress later empowered the Corps to remove snags and other obstacles to navigation in the Mississippi River. Other navigation projects followed, including locks and, after the Civil War, canals.

Corps engineers also surveyed and explored the new lands of the western United States and helped improve navigation in waterways. The Corps' official presence in the Pacific Northwest began in 1871 with the opening of an office in Portland, Oregon, still the headquarters for the region today. Work focused mainly on the Columbia and Willamette Rivers and the elimination or bypass of rapids. Early projects around Puget Sound addressed snag removal in the rivers and harbors. With the increased workload, the Corps opened an office in Seattle in 1896. Captain Harry Taylor was the first Seattle District engineer. According to William Willingham's history of the Corps in Seattle, "Army Engineers regarded a posting to Seattle as something less than a highlight of an officer's career," mostly because of the office's isolation from other Corps engineers.

The Army Corps of Engineers snagboat *W. T. Preston* clears a massive stump from a Seattle-area waterway.

Chin Gee Hee in his office, circa 1904.

CHINESE LABOR CONTRACTORS

Chinese laborers were essential to the growth of early Seattle. Beginning in the late 1860s, they generally hired out for hard manual-labor jobs throughout the region. They graded Seattle streets, laid tracks for the Northern Pacific and Great Northern railroads, built the Front Street cable line, mined coal, and worked on farms and in canneries. In the earliest years, most were employed by the Wa Chong Company, run by Chun Ching Hock and Chin Gee Hee. Chun Ching Hock started the company as a general merchandise store but soon expanded into labor contracting—mostly run by his partner— eventually becoming the largest labor supplier in Washington.

Both men became wealthy and owned extensive property in the city. Chin Gee Hee is credited with constructing the first brick building following Seattle's Great Fire of 1889. They were friends with many of the most influential citizens in Seattle, including Burke and Henry Yesler. Burke once said, "Seattle can point to no business career of higher honor, and few of more value to it, than that of Chin Gee Hee."

But such acclaim did not help the vast majority of Chinese living in Seattle. Deep-seated prejudice and growing resentment of the Chinese by out-of-work whites fueled some of the most reprehensible riots in the area's history. Mobs in Tacoma began to force most of the Chinese workers out of town in November 1885. The same mob violence occurred in October in Seattle and again in February 1886. By the end of the month, Chin Gee Hee and his family were some of the few Chinese still remaining in Seattle. There is no record of Chinese laborers ever working on the canals again.

between Lake Washington and Lake Union, and Lake Union and Salmon Bay. On June 6, 1883, the *Seattle P-I* reported that J. J. Cummings and Co. had won the bid to dig the canals. They would employ 100 men and many teams of horses. Reflecting growing racism among some in Seattle, Cummings promised that he would not hire any Chinese laborers.

Cummings began work on June 16 and kept up a rapid pace by adding more men and teams throughout the summer. In July, his crews removed 14,000 cubic yards of material for a canal connecting the two lakes at the location of the modern State Route 520. But then the men ran into the glacially deposited hardpan. When Cummings asked for more money than he had initially bid for sediment removal, the Improvement Company rejected his demand. In October, they abrogated his contract and hired Chinese labor through the contracting firm Wa Chong. For the canal they would open a cut three-quarters of a mile long, 10 feet deep, and 20 to 30 feet wide between Lake Union and Salmon Bay.

By March 1884, Wa Chong's men had advanced from Salmon Bay to within 50 yards of the lake but were forced to stop work by a court case brought by David Denny's Western Mill company. Considering the fact that Denny was also an investor in the canal project, it seems a bit strange that he would then, in essence, be suing himself with this case, but perhaps he finally realized that the canal would lower Lake Union and make his mill inoperable. The only way Wa Chong's crew could complete the job was to follow the court's restraining order to build "sufficient locks, gates, or dams" to keep the lake at its "ordinary natural level."

Looking east in the cut between Portage Bay and Union Bay, circa 1885.

A canoe heads from Portage Bay eastward through the cut in 1911.

Beyond these details, what Wa Chong's men did and when is not clear. Most of the information that exists comes from later sources. The crews probably finished digging the Fremont Cut sometime in 1885. Contemporary accounts describe their work on the canal from Salmon Bay to Lake Union, but there is no firsthand evidence as to whether they worked on the Montlake Portage between the lakes, even though it makes sense to assume that they did complete the job started by Cummings. The one clue that points to this outcome is a letter written in 1903 by engineer Eugene Ricksecker, who noted that he remembered seeing Chinese workers using picks and wheelbarrows at the cut. (A newspaper account suggests that whoever finished the work on the Portage did not do so until 1887.)

The connection between the lakes, known as the Portage canal, was wide enough for logs and small vessels. A report written in 1903 by John M. Clapp, a career engineer for the Army Corps of Engineers who interviewed more than a half dozen longtime residents, noted that the canal was 16 feet wide with vertical walls. Photographs from the era show a narrow cleft, crossed by a rickety-looking pedestrian bridge.

Clapp wrote that two locks, each 51 feet long, were able to lift small boats and steamers up to the larger lake and that the *City of Latona*, *Latona*, and *D.T. Denny* went from lake to lake in 1894. (Clapp, curiously, was the only one who provided specific

Opposite page:

Top: The lock at the lower, or Portage Bay, end of the cut, circa 1890.

Bottom: Looking west from Union Bay into the cut, circa 1890.

information about the locks. Another Corps report in 1890 simply noted that there were locks, without details of size.) The locks were located at the west end of the cut on the shore of Portage Bay.

When the channel between the lakes first opened, lumber rafts could pass through, but the logs damaged the locks, which resulted in the construction of a log chute, or raceway, that branched off from the main canal at its western end. The logs being transported via the raceway could be massive. In 1904, Frank Hergert of the Brace & Hergert Mill Co., which had taken over Denny's mill on Lake Union, wrote to the Corps requesting that the gates at the Montlake Portage be widened. He noted in a letter that at six feet nine inches wide, the locks were not big enough for "some of the larger logs." After their construction, the locks and raceway were kept closed except when transporting boats or logs.

Clapp believed that the main reason for the canal was not transportation but to allow David Denny to bring logs from Lake Washington to his mill on the smaller lake. Clapp further thought that the Lake Washington Improvement Company hoped to sell the canal system to the U.S. government, which is why they had the Wa Chong laborers open up a canal to Salmon Bay.

The federal government showed no interest in buying the LWIC canal, but in September 1890, Congress did provide $10,000 to form a three-member board of engineers—Colonel George H. Mendell, Major Thomas H. Handbury, and Captain Thomas W. Symons—who would study a canal "to connect Lakes Union, Samamish (sic), and Washington with Puget Sound." They then hired Philip G. Eastwick to conduct the survey. His report and the board's report went to Brigadier General Thomas Casey of the Corps, who submitted a summary document to the Secretary of War in December 1891.

Mendell's report dismissed any sort of canal from Lake Sammamish to Lake Washington and focused

instead on five possible routes to connect Lake Washington to Puget Sound. Route one followed the natural link of the Duwamish and Black Rivers. The second and third were Alexander's tramway and Mercer's Farm routes to Lake Union. The final two routes utilized Salmon Bay, with one connecting to it via Shilshole Bay and the other going from Elliott Bay through Smith Cove (today's Interbay). Mendell rejected the Duwamish route because of its great cost and eliminated Alexander's routes because the landscape had changed in 20 years; what had been wilderness was now built up with businesses, which also raised the price of procuring the right-of-way. (In just the previous two years, from 1889 to 1891, Seattle had grown in population from 36,655 to 50,583. Most of the growth came immediately after Seattle's Great Fire of June 6, 1889, which led to a wholesale rebuilding of the downtown and the relocation of most of the city's lumber mills to Lake Union and Salmon Bay.)

Of the final two routes, Mendell preferred going through Smith Cove because its entrance was closer to the main Seattle harbor and was "less exposed to bombardment by an enemy's fleet." It was, however, more expensive, $3.5 million compared to $2.9 million for the Shilshole route. Both routes would keep Lake Union and Lake Washington at their present levels. One set of locks would raise and lower boats between Puget Sound and Salmon Bay, and another between the two lakes.

Mendell also listed several reasons why the canal and locks were necessary. They would open up miles of freshwater shoreline for commercial facilities free from the influence of tides. Freshwater would also eliminate the dreaded teredos, shipworms that destroyed docks and pilings in a matter of months.

Right: This postcard from the 1910s shows the lumber mill in the Fremont neighborhood at the outlet of Lake Union, and the gate system to the channel out to Salmon Bay.

Shingle mills in Ballard produced more shingles than any other location on Earth. In the foreground is the train trestle across Salmon Bay.

A Bird's Eye View of Fremont, Woodland Park in distance.

PHOTO BY NOWELL & ROGNON.

With a federal survey completed, the means to create a canal seemed imminent, or so Seattleites thought. Daniel Gilman, who helped to develop the Seattle, Lake Shore and Eastern Railway, wrote to LWIC cofounder Thomas Burke that a canal bill before Congress had the backing of the state delegation. Gilman added that James Hill, owner of the Great Northern Railway, would work to convince congressional Democrats—who were the weakest supporters—of the merits of the canal. Locally, the *Seattle P-I* ran numerous articles trumpeting the project with statements such as the opening of the canal would lead to Lake Washington becoming "the finest and most convenient fresh-water harbor in the world."

Not everyone in the state supported the idea of a locks and canal system or of federal money going to Seattle. In particular, the state Democratic Party opposed what they called the "Seattle Ditch." Driven by Pierce County, the representatives from rural counties at the party's convention in Olympia were "practically unanimous in their denunciation of the Lake Washington canal scheme," according to the *Tacoma Daily News*. The reason was simple: money from the federal government could be better spent on other projects outside Seattle.

In contrast, the Republican Party included a pro-canal statement in their party plank, and in the 1892 election for governor, their candidate John McGraw won, in part because of his "Dig the Ditch" stance. Unfortunately, it was too late, as Congress, sensing the anti-canal sentiment from around the state, refused to provide any additional funding for a canal in the 1892 River and Harbor Act. Once again, it seemed as if Seattleites would have to wait for their canal. But a new canal proposal was already in the works. This one, however, would not connect Puget Sound to Lake Washington via Lake Union. Instead it would be south of downtown Seattle and link Elliott Bay directly to Lake Washington through a deep chasm in Beacon Hill.

Lumber and shingle mills in
Ballard used Salmon Bay as a sort
of mill pond, but the salt water
exposed the logs to burrowing
organisms if left too long.

*If we make suitable efforts and have
a little patience this great work will be
accomplished. But we become impatient
at long and vexatious delays, especially in
such hard times as these, and many, losing
their mental balance, become reckless, and
are ready to indorse or engage in any wild
scheme that may be presented by political
demagogues or financial speculators.*

– JOHN J. McGILVRA TO EDITOR, *SEATTLE P-I*, JULY 15, 1894

CHAPTER 3

Routing and Funding

The mastermind behind what would be called the south canal was Eugene Semple. A former newspaper editor in Oregon and territorial governor of Washington, he was a classic frontier entrepreneur, always ready with the next great scheme to make money in a new way in a new land. One year after Washington achieved statehood in 1889, Governor Ferry appointed Semple to the state Harbor Line Commission. The state legislature had convened the commission to determine inner and outer harbor lines for the navigable bays, lakes, and rivers adjacent to incorporated cities and towns. Semple was assigned to work on Seattle's harbor, which allowed him to become familiar with its characteristics and potential as a port.

He quickly began to develop a new scheme—a canal connecting Lake Washington with Elliott Bay. One possible route ran along Pine Street, which was then at the northern reaches of the business district, but he also envisioned a second canal route in an 1891 proposal that involved dredging a pair of waterways into the estuary at the mouth of the Duwamish River. These would link to a canal across Beacon Hill to Lake Washington. Sediment from that canal would then be used to fill in the tideflats in the eastern side of Elliott Bay, in the area now known as SODO.

Semple does not appear to have pursued the canal project immediately. It was only after the passage of a state law allowing private companies to construct waterways across tidelands and collect payment via liens on land created by the spoils that he moved forward with his plan for Elliott Bay. Although his biographer Alan Hynding wrote that Semple's role in the bill was "not known," a later promotional publication for the south canal project credited Semple with drafting the bill that was introduced into the state House of Representatives by Seattle representatives Will R. White and Luthene C. Gilman. Their bill passed the legislature with remarkably little opposition or fanfare in February 1893. It is surprising that "Dig the Ditch" governor John McGraw signed the bill, given that it would be put to use to disrupt plans for the north canal, but it's likely that he did not envision the canal element of Semple's plan and saw it only as a tidelands filling bill.

The bill established a process by which waterway developers could file a plan delineating the location of a waterway across tidelands and identifying which lands would be filled. Once accepted by the

This detail from Alfred B. Burr's 1884 illustration of Seattle shows the southern end of Elliott Bay. Semple's plan involved cutting a canal from here all the way to Lake Washington and filling the tideflats to create more waterfront.

commissioner of public lands, the proposal had to be approved by the governor. Semple altered his 1891 proposal slightly and submitted it on June 8, 1893, to Commissioner of Public Lands William T. Forrest, who approved it and sent it to Governor McGraw. McGraw, seeing the canal element of the plan and likely realizing the implications of the project for the north canal, held on to the contract for more than a year before signing it.

While waiting for the contract to be signed, Semple incorporated the Seattle and Lake Washington Waterway Company (SLWWC) on June 25, 1894. In addition to former governor Elisha P. Ferry, who was named president, a number of other Seattle businessmen helped form the company, including wealthy meat packer Charles Frye, former city engineer Albro Gardner, and Andrew Hemrich, president of Seattle Brewing and Malting Company. Semple served as vice president, and Captain Thomas Symons of the Corps signed on as the consulting engineer for the project. Symons' involvement is puzzling. Corps policies did not prevent him from working for the SLWWC, but it did have a taint of conflict of interest, particularly given that he received shares of capital stock in the company.

At that moment it certainly seemed unlikely that the federal project for a north canal would proceed. As one SLWWC director gloated to another in November 1894, "I just had a talk with [newspaper publisher] Tom Prosch about the north canal. He said that he had given up being able to do anything with it as it would cost over $300000 for Right of Way damages to property and servey (sic). He thinks that it now depends on our company to give Seattle a Ship Canal. This settles the question of the North Canal and we will have no further trouble from them." Nothing could have been further from the truth. The contest for public support and federal funding was just beginning.

In 1894, McGilvra opened the attack on Semple, writing in a letter to the *Seattle P-I* editor, "The

EUGENE SEMPLE

Eugene Semple had a varied career, like many of his fellow emigrants from the Midwest. Born in 1840 in Bogotá, Colombia, where his father served at the American consulate as the chargé d'affaires, and raised in Illinois, he moved to Oregon Territory in 1863. Semple practiced law, edited the Democratic paper in Portland, the *Oregon Herald*, and owned the Lucia mill, across the border in Vancouver, Washington. None of these endeavors were particularly successful. President Grover Cleveland, a Democrat, repaid Semple for his work for the Party with an appointment as Washington's territorial governor in 1887. When Washington gained statehood in 1889, Semple threw his hat in the ring during the first gubernatorial race, but lost to Elisha P. Ferry. After losing control of the Seattle and Lake Washington Waterway Company in 1905, Semple tried to interest the federal government in a scheme to bypass the treacherous Columbia River bar by building a canal from Astoria to Seaside, in Oregon. This scheme, too, failed, and he died in San Diego in 1908, at the age of 68.

canal feature of this scheme is not only not practicable on account of the enormous cost of the work, but it is evidently a blind to catch the ear and eye of the public and divert attention from the real purpose of this waterway company." Others, such as Arthur Denny and Thomas Burke, also questioned Semple's motives.

Foremost among many arguments was the scale and potential complications of Semple's plan. Was it even feasible given that the canal would have 308-foot-tall walls sloping outward from the channel? Semple insisted that the banks would be stable because the cut would be perpendicular to the layers of clay, sand, and till deposited by glaciers. The more vulnerable surfaces on the east and west would be left undisturbed. Tellingly, he didn't address the question of how the chasm would be crossed by streets, streetcars, and pipelines.

The SLWWC countered the opposition by filing a water right on Lake Washington in August 1894. The acquisition of this right may have indicated that Semple intended to cut a canal and use the water moving through it to generate power. It also may have been an effort to limit the north canal project because the right could be used to block any attempts to lower Lake Washington.

At about the same time, Congress stepped back into the project by appropriating $25,000 for a survey of the north canal project. The expenditure was contingent upon acquisition by King County of the canal right-of-way and transfer of the land to the federal government, along with a release from damages from any changes to water levels.

The Chamber of Commerce, led by Edward O. Graves, sought a middle ground between the competing proposals because Semple's plan offered a method for filling in the tidelands and creating much-needed level land along the waterfront. Graves told a *Seattle P-I* reporter:

I think that the public mind has been somewhat divided and confused by the fact that another

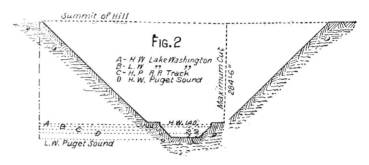

Cross-section of Semple's proposed canal through Beacon Hill as shown in an 1895 *Engineering Record* article.

waterway is projected to the south of the city. There is no necessary conflict between the two propositions. One is a public and the other is a private enterprise. If the government once begins work under its plan, there need be no fear that it will stop work because private parties have planned an entirely different project. . . . The primary object of their scheme is to secure earth with which to fill up the tide flats, and, as I understand it, they expect to derive their profit not so much from the canal itself as from the reclamation of the tide flats.

He seemed to be indicating that he never expected the south canal to Lake Washington to open anyway. It appears that Graves and others assumed that Semple concocted the canal plan only to make it possible to sluice enough land down from the hillside to fill the tideflats because dredging would not provide enough spoils to fill the vast acreage in the bay.

The following March, the federal government allowed $5,000 of the earlier appropriation to be spent for an initial survey of the north canal. In addition to identifying the right-of-way, Captain Symons and his assistant Eugene Ricksecker, who completed the survey in August 1895, primarily straightened and shortened the various canal routes proposed in 1891.

In order to get the release of the remaining federal funding, the King County Board of Commissioners passed a resolution authorizing the acquisition of the canal right-of-way in 1895. The county was exercising a new power that the state legislature had granted

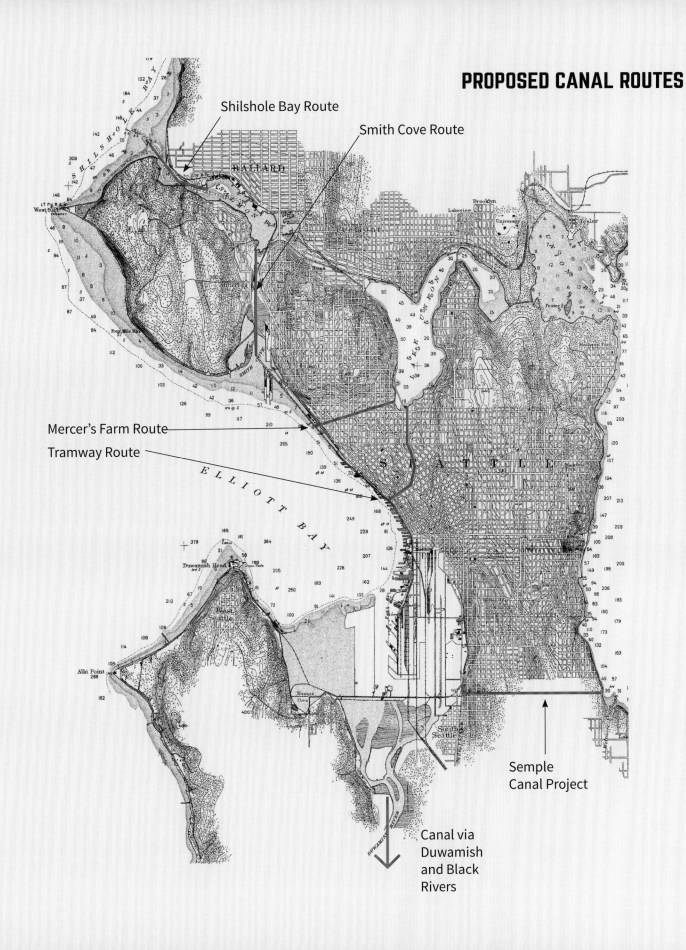

PROPOSED CANAL ROUTES

Shilshole Bay Route

Smith Cove Route

Mercer's Farm Route

Tramway Route

Semple
Canal Project

Canal via
Duwamish
and Black
Rivers

Top to bottom:
John J. McGilvra, Judge
Roger S. Greene, and
Judge Thomas Burke.

MCGILVRA, GREENE, AND BURKE

Of all the Seattleites involved in the decades of effort to build the Lake Washington Ship Canal, three civic leaders outpaced the others in terms of longevity and fervor: John J. McGilvra, Judge Roger S. Greene, and Judge Thomas Burke. All were lawyers, all from east of the Mississippi, and all deeply involved in civic affairs. They worked together for decades to propel the ship canal project forward by raising funds, writing and promoting favorable legislation, lobbying Congress, and prodding the Army Corps of Engineers. They also organized meetings and railed against Semple's canal scheme to increase public support for the northern route. Greene was the most directly involved, serving as chair of the Chamber's Lake Washington Canal committee for 20 years.

Although the trio stood to gain financially, civic responsibility played a central role in their fervor, and each had a long history of civic work. McGilvra served as U.S. Attorney, advanced efforts to construct a Snoqualmie Pass road, garnered public support for the Cedar River water system, and helped establish the King County Bar Association. Burke served on the school board, was involved in newspaper publishing, and was one of the incorporators of the Seattle, Lake Shore and Eastern Railway, Seattle's answer to the malfeasance of the Northern Pacific. Greene served as Chief Justice of the territorial Supreme Court, successfully lobbied for the inclusion of a public library in the 1890 city charter, and helped establish the Wayside Mission Hospital.

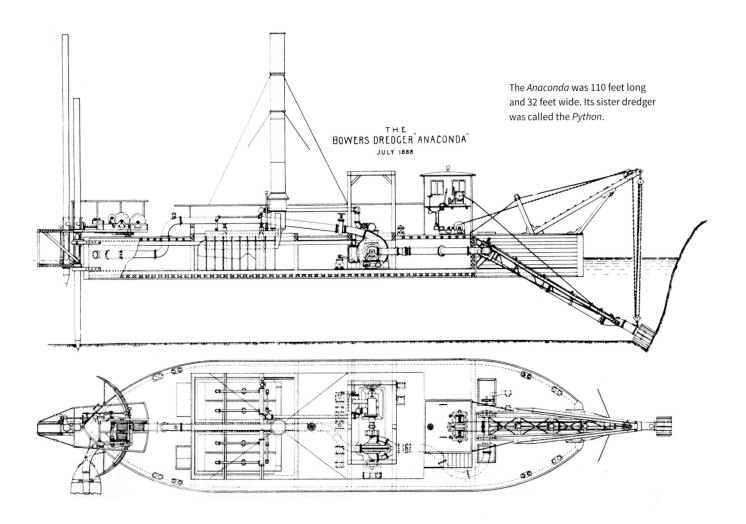

THE
BOWERS DREDGER "ANACONDA"
JULY 1888

The *Anaconda* was 110 feet long and 32 feet wide. Its sister dredger was called the *Python*.

to counties to carry out public works projects, condemn lands as needed, and impose levies to fund those projects.

Meanwhile, the SLWWC had begun to raise private funds for its south canal and tidelands fill project. The Mississippi Valley Trust Company, of St. Louis, which had connections to Semple's wealthy nephews, agreed to finance the canal's construction, but like the federal government, they wanted proof that local residents supported the canal project, and required a $500,000 subsidy. Luckily, they only required a pledge of the subsidy, to be paid upon completion of the canal. A pledge was much easier to acquire than an actual investment during the recession that lingered after the Panic of 1893.

Seeking to garner financial support from Seattleites, the SLWWC held a public meeting on

March 28, 1895. With speeches from the mayor and other prominent citizens, Semple's company raised the first $100,300 on the spot from the 3,500 attendees. By May 10, $545,000 had been pledged, and work began on July 29, when Eugene Semple's daughter Zoe set the machinery on the dredger *Anaconda* in motion with the lift of a lever.

By the summer of 1895, Seattle had two partially funded canal projects. One was arguably a front for a tidelands fill scheme, and the other would require considerable lobbying to secure federal funding for full construction. It was highly unlikely that both could be built. At the very least, not enough water flowed out of Lake Washington for the operation of two separate locks. Also, Congress, having located the naval shipyard at Bremerton in 1890, did not have a compelling military reason to build the canal. It was apparent, too, that Elliott Bay would have sufficient space for the volume of trade passing through the port for at least the immediate future.

Once the SLWWC began moving ahead with the St. Louis investors' funding, McGilvra and 14 other north canal supporters, including City Engineer Reginald H. Thomson, wrote to the Secretary of War Daniel S. Lamont on August 15, 1895, asking for the replacement of Captain Symons because of the conflict of interest between his work for the SLWWC and the Corps of Engineers. The letter minced no words: "The private undertaking is calculated and intended to delay and defeat the Government Canal and to that end and for that purpose this private corporation 'The Lake Washington Canal and Waterway Company' (sic) have employed Captain Thomas W. Symons, as their Engineer in Chief and he has been and now is one of the chief promotors (sic) of this opposition scheme." McGilvra added that if the north canal project was canceled, it was more likely that the south canal promoters could get federal funding and accused Symons of delaying his survey of the north canal.

Lamont appears to have listened. Symons completed the north canal survey shortly after this skirmish and was then transferred to Buffalo. He continued to correspond with Semple until at least 1901, giving him advice on the machinations of the federal government and gaining support for the south canal.

But the battle was hardly over. Between 1895 and 1897, supporters of each canal tried different tactics to ensure that their canal would get built. The Chamber of Commerce threw its support behind the north canal. Judge Greene of the Chamber sent stacks of telegrams and letters to Senator Watson Squire, who was working in Washington, D.C., to increase federal investment in the north canal. They coordinated efforts to get appropriations in the River and Harbor acts, the annual spending bills that funded Corps waterway work. In addition, McGilvra prodded Squire to get the Secretary of the Army to decide whether the canal would connect with Puget Sound via Shilshole Bay or Smith Cove.

The Chamber also rallied public support for the northern route. On April 19, 1896, at a public meeting at the Armory, those present passed a resolution condemning the SLWWC canal. It dismissed the very idea of a south canal, stating that "nature has provided a route and only one proper route, for a ship canal to connect the saltwater harbor of Seattle with its fresh water harbors of Lake Union and Washington over which route the waters of Lake Washington now find their way to the sea through Lake Union."

Connecting Lake Washington (far right) to salt water via Lake Union was the most logical choice to north canal supporters, as this 1904 bird's eye view shows. Supporters, however, were divided on where the cut should go from Lake Union to salt water.

LAKE UNION

Lawsuits filed the following summer by tideland owners against the SLWWC also took their toll. Although the claims were eventually decided in favor of the company, the dredging contractor, Bowers Dredging Company, went into receivership in the summer of 1896, which halted work on the south canal.

The north canal made another step forward in 1898, when the debate over its canal outlet was finally resolved. Canal supporters wanted it to run through the trough of land between Magnolia and Queen Anne Hill to Smith Cove on Elliott Bay, but this put them at odds with the Great Northern Railway Company. The railroad opposed the route because the canal would occupy space adjacent to its rail yard located to the south of Salmon Bay and its two large docks in Smith Cove.

The Great Northern normally enjoyed the support and affection of Seattleites. In 1893, it was the first transcontinental railroad to locate its terminus in Seattle. Then, in 1896, it inaugurated regular transpacific service to the city in partnership with the Nippon Yusen Kaisha Line. By 1898, however, the railroad's decision to oppose the Smith Cove route led to strong criticism. McGilvra wrote to the Board of Engineers then studying the canal routes to complain, "The Great Northern is a white blackbird in the flock, but we have not had a benevolent monopoly since Henry Villard's time. They all want the earth, and some of them would like the moon and stars thrown in. They have secured control of the entire front of our saltwater harbor, and now object to be disturbed by this canal to connect it with our fresh water harbors."

The *Seattle Times* also vented its anger at the possible change of route, editorializing, "This would seem ludicrous were it not for the fact that aggregated capital and corporate power is fast encroaching upon the rights and liberties of the people, and assuming to control the functions of Government."

A *Seattle P-I* article took a more level approach, citing the various factors at play in the decision resulting from a meeting between the Board of Engineers, the Great Northern, and representatives of the Chamber of Commerce on March 15, 1898. First, the Smith Cove canal entrance would be exposed to Seattle's strongest winds, which come from the southwest in the winter. Second, the route

The Great Northern's Oriental Limited passing by the company's Smith Cove docks, circa 1905.

Opposite page:
Sediment sucked up by the *Anaconda* and *Python* traveled through pipes and was deposited on the Elliott Bay tideflats until the ground surface was two feet above high tide line.

between Shilshole Bay and the Fremont Cut would be straighter than a path from the northern outlet of a Smith Cove cut. Furthermore, test piles (logs driven into the ground to assess soil conditions) hit quicksand below the seemingly solid ground at Smith Cove, whereas the Shilshole Bay location provided a compacted glacial till foundation for the locks. The Shilshole Bay route may have entailed further travel from Elliott Bay, but it saved $250,000 in excavation and related costs. Finally, although the Great Northern was not currently using the full width of the level land between the bays, building a canal would limit their long-term plans for the area and impact Seattle's port operations.

In April 1898, the Secretary of War approved the Board of Engineers' plan to follow the Shilshole Bay route, with the locks located at the Narrows, or western edge, of Salmon Bay. Condemnations proceeded and by later that year, all rights had been acquired, which included payments to the shoreline owners on Salmon Bay for land that would be inundated by the rising waters. The federal government accepted the deeded lands in 1900. The Washington state legislature then passed a bill on February 5, 1901, releasing the federal government from any liability related to the raising or lowering of waterbodies resulting from the canal's construction. Once the federal government accepted the land, it had essentially committed to building the canal.

The Corps began by clearing the site of the locks at the Narrows between Salmon Bay and Shilshole Bay, installing tide gauges at the lock site, and boring seabed samples to assess the soil conditions along the canal right-of-way and at the lock site. In May 1901, a narrow cut between Salmon Bay and Lake Union was authorized. The Corps' 1901 annual report explained, "Its object is to place the control of the outlet from Lake Union in the hands of the Government—the present outlet being through a small creek flowing partly through private property—to determine the nature of the

material to be excavated and the cost, and to hasten the adjustment of questions of street and railroad crossings and the disposition of material that will be excavated from the full canal section." By 1902, 4,300 feet of the cut would be made to a depth of 16 feet above low water.

To the south, the SLWWC doggedly continued its efforts to fill tidelands and begin work on its canal. In 1900 it received an extension on its contract with the state and was able to attract funding from Morris & Whitehead, New York bankers. By late 1901, 175 acres of new land had been created by the dredging of the East Waterway. The next year, the SLWWC negotiated a deal with the city for discounted rates on water from the Cedar River water system, which they would use to sluice sediments off Beacon Hill and down into the tideflats.

The two canal plans were once again on a collision course. Part of the reason that both groups of canal proponents were able to continue fighting for their projects was the booming Seattle economy. On July 17, 1897, the steamship *Portland* had arrived in Seattle carrying more than a ton of gold from the

Klondike. Seattle quickly became the biggest economic beneficiary, primarily as supplier of the "ton of provisions" that every miner needed, which resulted in a huge increase in manufacturing and shipping. By 1900, the population had grown to 80,671, and by 1910, more than 235,000 people lived in the city. The influx of people and capital into the economy jump-started development and sustained it into the next decade, which helped solidify Seattle's long-term connection with Alaska.

Crowds on the Seattle waterfront as ships depart for Alaska and the Klondike Gold Rush, 1898.

In order to promote their projects, both Semple and several north canal supporters traveled to Washington, D.C., in March 1901 to address the House Rivers and Harbors Committee. The bickering and discord dampened the committee's enthusiasm for the government canal project, and they appropriated only $160,000 for it. To the dismay of the Chamber and other north canal supporters, the act also ordered another study of the canal projects. McGilvra wrote to the newest Board of Engineers, "This act is a surprise to us, and is no doubt one of those congressional accidents not uncommon." His disbelief that the south canal could be seriously considered lay in his certainty that "as to this other proposed line, we had believed and still believe it to be a myth."

The Board of Engineers, led by Lieutenant Colonel William H. Heuer, reported to the Chief of Engineers in 1902 that the south canal was technically feasible but "almost impracticable," considering the amount of material to be excavated and the number of streets, railroads, and other city infrastructure that already crossed it or would cross it in the future. The north canal, on the other hand, was "entirely feasible," but the board questioned whether the benefits would justify the costs for construction, maintenance, and operation. Looking at the region, the engineers saw that enough land was already available to be developed, timber was still plentiful and cheap enough to make replacing teredo-riddled piers reasonable, and trains carried coal to the port with little difficulty.

The 1902 report's conclusions do not appear to have hampered work on either canal project. The lack of support expressed by the Board of Engineers is belied by the work done by the Corps over the next few years. They built a small office building at the Narrows; finished the preliminary cut between Salmon Bay and Lake Union; built a temporary gate at the head of the Fremont Cut; cleared the lock site at the Montlake Portage; approved a plan and the location for the Northern Pacific train bridge; installed three 30-inch siphons at the Montlake Cut, improving its drainage capacity; and dredged a turning basin at the outlet of the Fremont Cut.

A few miles to the south, on Elliott Bay, the SLWWC began carving the canal out of Beacon Hill in November 1901. By late 1904, crews had used hydraulic giants—technology used in the California and Klondike gold rushes—to wash seven blocks down to the tideflats, creating 52 acres of new land, but also leaving houses perched precariously at the edge of the muddy maw.

The north canal supporters used this against the company. They began a campaign protesting the use of city water for the south canal project, pointing out that the City of Ballard had been denied the use of Cedar River water even when they were willing to pay full price. Civic leaders like Horace Cayton, publisher of the *Seattle Republican*, encouraged the City Council to protect the interests of the city: "There is no more probability of the 'south canal' ever being put through so that ships can pass through it than there is of Puget Sound being drained for a farm. . . . The plot was conceived in sin and brought forth in iniquity, and the city council acts wisely in squelching the life out of it."

Although Semple's south canal was never completed, the hydraulic cannons took a huge bite out of Beacon Hill, which created the gap where South Columbian Way now accesses the hill.

HIRAM CHITTENDEN

Brigadier General Hiram M. Chittenden spent just over a decade in Seattle, but had a tremendous influence on the city and the region. Born in 1858 in New York, Chittenden graduated from West Point and joined the Army Corps of Engineers. He served in Yellowstone National Park and was assigned to numerous river projects, including the Missouri River Commission. By the time he moved to Seattle, he had reached the rank of major. While commander of the Seattle District he would be promoted to lieutenant colonel, just prior to when he stepped down, in September 1908. His replacement was Charles W. Kutz.

While moving up the ranks and around the country, Chittenden also delved into the history of the American West. He wrote a two-volume work, *The American Fur Trade of the Far West*, published in 1902; a history of Yellowstone National Park in 1904; and *Life, Letters and Travels of Father Pierre-Jean de Smet, S.J., 1801-1873* in 1905.

He did not restrict his work in Seattle to the Lake Washington Ship Canal. Chittenden studied flooding problems in the Duwamish-Green River Valley and helped Everett resolve its harbor issues. Further afield, in Aberdeen, he engineered a solution to help narrow the Grays Harbor channel and use the movement of water to keep it clear.

In January 1910, Chittenden was promoted to brigadier general. He retired the next month, due to ongoing health problems, which however did not prevent him from running for and winning a position on the newly formed Port of Seattle Commission. He served on the commission from 1911 to 1915, including two terms as president. As an engineer, he brought his expertise to the development of a comprehensive plan for the port, including Fishermen's Terminal.

To honor Chittenden, the locks at Ballard were named for him in 1956 for the role he played in bringing the canal project to fruition.

The campaign worked. The City Council canceled SLWWC's contract to use city water as of June 13, 1904. This was the end of the south canal scheme. (The area where Semple's canal began is still visible; it's the cleft in Beacon Hill where South Columbian Way goes from Interstate 5 up to Beacon Hill.) Though stopped in its canal plans, the SLWWC continued filling tidelands. By 1917, they had made about 1,400 acres of new land, including Harbor Island, and excavated the East and West Waterways through the estuary at the mouth of the Duwamish River. That year, the commissioner of public lands refused to extend the company's contract and it expired on July 1, 1917, just three days before the official dedication of the Ballard Locks.

In 1906, fearing that Congress might not fully fund the canal in the near future, the Chamber of Commerce endorsed a new plan. James A. Moore, a developer who built residential neighborhoods, the Moore Theater, and several downtown office buildings during his career, had a group of East Coast investors interested in building a steel plant on Lake Washington. They would need access to Puget Sound, so Moore proposed that King County pay him $500,000 to construct a timber lock and dredge the channel. A committee of three Chamber trustees—Burke, McGraw, and former state senator Frederick C. Harper—reviewed the proposal and recommended that the Chamber endorse the plan, with the condition that the lock be built at the Narrows and that payment be withheld until the canal was complete.

Congress granted Moore permission in June 1906, the King County Commissioners approved the plan in August, voters approved the issuance of bonds in September, and preparations for construction began. Why did Congress approve Moore's proposal so easily? It appears that Moore and McGraw went to Washington, D.C., for the vote and personally struck a deal with the Corps' Chief of Engineers General Alexander Mackenzie, promising to operate the locks for three years before handing them over to the Corps. Representative Hiram Burton, Republican from Delaware and chair of the House Rivers and Harbors Committee, agreed not to oppose the bill when he realized that it relieved the federal government of the cost of constructing the locks.

A surprising element of the scheme is found in a series of letters in Eugene Semple's papers. They indicate that he played a role in this canal scheme, too. In May 1907, Moore wrote to Semple, "The Canal will no doubt be built, Governor, but had you and I not taken up the matter from a business standpoint, it is safe to say that the canal would not have been constructed as it was absolutely lost in politics."

Even with congressional approval and county funding seemingly arranged, Moore did not get to build the canal. In April 1906, Major Hiram M. Chittenden replaced Lieutenant Francis A. Pope as the head of the Seattle District of the Corps and began to study the situation at the request of General Mackenzie. Chittenden was concerned that the timber lock proposed in Moore's scheme would be insufficient and the government would end up inheriting an inadequate facility.

According to historian William F. Willingham, Chittenden started a behind-the-scenes campaign to discount Moore's plan and turn public opinion toward finding funding for a masonry lock, to be built by the Corps. Aiding Chittenden was the Lake Washington Canal Association, a group led by Burke, McGraw, and Greene, which formed in the spring of 1907 to promote the canal and development around it. Moore transferred his canal rights to the association, and the state legislature authorized it to collect assessments and expend them under the supervision of the district engineer to build a canal. Congress passed legislation in March 1907 to allow the local group to excavate the canal only, relieving them of the responsibility of building the locks.

Chittenden filed his report with Mackenzie on December 6, 1907. In it, he explained the need for a

Hiram M. Chittenden, circa 1916.

Below: Roger S. Greene and other investors didn't expect to strike it rich with their investments, instead using the association to further their larger goals for the city.

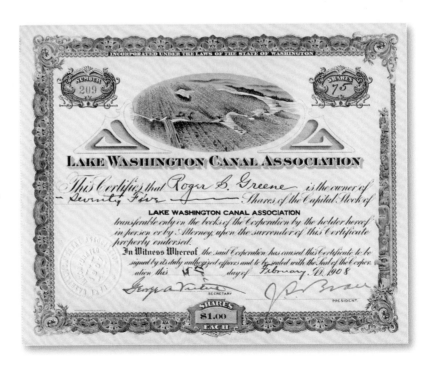

masonry lock at the mouth of Salmon Bay, at the Narrows. He also recommended construction of two locks at that site, one for larger ships and another for smaller vessels. He added another set of gates to the large lock, too, so it could accommodate midsize vessels without having to fill the entire large lock. Perhaps more significantly, Chittenden eliminated the Montlake lock entirely as a cost-saving measure, which would result in Lake Washington being lowered to the level of Lake Union. Chittenden had recently produced a report that addressed the flood problems that had long upset residents in the Duwamish-Green River valley. Part of his solution involved shifting the Cedar River into the lake and eliminating the Black River entirely.

Chittenden's plan for the Seattle locks faced two hurdles before construction would begin: locating the locks and funding their construction.

Some Ballard mill owners had long favored locating the locks at the head of Salmon Bay (i.e., the outlet of the Fremont Cut) rather than at the Narrows (the present location), because a flooded Salmon Bay would force them to move and/or raise their docks. They now organized for one final attempt to preserve the status quo. (Some mill men even suggested washing Queen Anne Hill down into Lake Union, to create more land for industry.) Arguing that the original condemnation in the 1890s did not cover the increase in land values in the ensuing decade, they added that it also did not cover the costs of raising the mills above the

Ballard mills line the north shore of Salmon Bay, 1903.

new water line. Although they had already been compensated for those damages, they claimed the long delay between the condemnation and construction had increased the costs of raising their docks. They were emboldened by assurances that the locks would be moved in return for their support of shorelands sale legislation. The Chamber of Commerce threw their support behind the new lock location and Chittenden also voiced his support, though his biographer, Gordon B. Dodds, asserted that he only did so with the idea of getting consensus and moving the project forward.

The lumber mill owners' opposition is curious given the rather elaborate transshipment required by the existing conditions, described by engineer Ricksecker in an 1895 letter: "Vessels loading from Salmon Bay are anchored in deep water of Puget Sound opposite the mouth of the bay 1.7 miles from the mills. Here they receive their cargoes from barges that have been previously loaded at the mills and towed alongside. The lumber shipped from Fremont Mill on Lake Union is loaded upon cars at the mill and switched to the Smith Cove dock, 3.6 miles by rail, and transshipped thence to vessels." Hiram Chittenden would later chide the mill owners that they just wanted to "spread logs around it [Salmon Bay] wherever they see fit, without regard to a free channel for shipping."

McGilvra and Washington senator Samuel H. Piles both continued to lobby members of Congress for the Narrows site. Chittenden shifted his position again, back to locating the locks at the Narrows. He also began to rally support locally by holding public meetings and writing articles for local newspapers. In February 1910, the *Seattle Times* reported that supporters of the Narrows location feared that if the location was changed, a new survey would have to be conducted and "Congress will become disgusted and do nothing."

Chittenden continued his lobbying on behalf of the canal even though he had retired as District Engineer for the Corps in 1908 due to ill health. He died in October 1917, not long after the locks were dedicated.

Logs moving up from Salmon Bay into the Seattle Cedar Lumber Mill via a conveyor belt, 1915. At low tide, floating log booms lay far below the deck of the mill's pier.

With the ship canal between Salmon Bay and Lake Union funded, digging began

In 1910, the Rivers and Harbors Act included a $2,275,000 appropriation for the ship canal. This allowed the project to proceed along the lines proposed by Chittenden. The Salmon Bay lumber mills apparently could not compete against the momentum created by the Rivers and Harbors Act funding.

Just two conditions had to be met: assumption of liability and canal excavation by King County. The King County Board of Commissioners and state Supreme Court resolved those two issues. The commissioners agreed to assume liability for the lowering of Lake Washington in May 1911. Then, one month later, the Washington state Supreme Court clarified the constitutionality of a portion of the funding plan.

In that same ruling, the court reversed an earlier court decision invalidating an act passed by the state legislators in March 1909 to allocate $250,000 to the canal project. The money was surplus from a sale of shorelands around Lake Union and Lake Washington to fund construction of the 1909 Alaska-Yukon-Pacific Exposition, and a quarter-million dollars had not been spent. Seattle legislator George Cotterill introduced a bill that put the money to work on the canal.

The bickering continued in Seattle and Washington, D.C., with much of the rancor rooted in the railroads' opposition to the plan because assessments would affect land they owned along the canal. A number of Seattleites went to Washington, D.C., in late June to lobby politicians and agency staff directly. Finally, on June 22, 1911, Secretary of War Henry Lewis Stimson called all of the factions into a daylong hearing to sort out the situation. John H. Powell, Joseph B. Alexander, and Alexander F. McEwan, all suspected agents of the railroads, spoke against the canal. Representative Will E. Humphrey and Judge Burke spoke for it. Their case was made stronger by the arrival of a telegram trumpeting the King County Commissioners' passage of a resolution pledging their willingness to use all legal means to fund the canal excavation. The following week, the state Supreme Court validated the commissioners' 1910 harbor bonds measure, which included $750,000 for excavation of the canal.

With concerns about local support and funding for the canal allayed, the Secretary of War approved the immediate start of work on the locks at the Narrows on June 29, 1911.

1909 STATE SHORE LAND IMPROVEMENT FUND

In their quest to secure funding for excavating the canal, the King County Commissioners and canal supporters went after any dollar they could unearth. Knowing that a balance remained from the $1 million appropriated for the construction of buildings and other expenses related to the Alaska-Yukon-Pacific Exposition, the commissioners sought to have the remaining funds allocated to canal construction.

The legislature agreed in March 1909, shifting the money from the exposition to the canal work and establishing the Shore Land Improvement Fund before the fair even opened in June. They put one condition on the funding: all soils excavated from the canal route had to be deposited either on the University of Washington grounds or on state-owned lands on Union Bay or Lake Union. In this way, the university and the state gained new land. Most of the sediment was deposited along the Union Bay shoreline of the university campus, adjacent to where Husky Stadium would be built in 1920. Recent studies have found that about 15 feet of dredged and excavated soils were deposited on the marshes in Union Bay.

Gantry crane and transport train on trestle in the locks pit, 1914.

CHAPTER 4

Building the Canal: 1909-1917

Although the debate over the funding and details of the canal continued for another two years, once the state funding from the sale of shorelands was available, the county's work could begin. It did so on October 27, 1909, with the first official excavation for the Lake Washington Ship Canal.

More than 500 people gathered on the cleared but undeveloped land between Lake Washington and Lake Union. To the north of the Montlake Portage was the University of Washington campus, where Seattle's first world's fair, the Alaska-Yukon-Pacific Exposition (AYP), had ended about two weeks earlier. A few hundred feet to the south was the narrow cut initially completed in 1885 and still primarily used for transporting logs to mills on Lake Union. Further south was mostly forested land and the 23rd Avenue Montlake line street trolley, which had opened in May to provide an easy route to the fairgrounds. The line ran for less than a year from downtown to the southern entrance to the AYP, a few hundred yards north of the modern canal.

Although the state was providing the money for canal excavation (from the shorelands sale), the Corps had announced in July that it would take over the construction of the canal and locks. They would do the work at the locks, and King County would be responsible for the Montlake and Fremont Cuts, under the auspices of the Corps. In

Above: Panorama view of (left
to right) Union Bay on Lake
Washington, Montlake, and
Portage Bay in 1909.

Below: Cofferdam surrounding
locks under construction,
August 23, 1914.

August, contractor C. J. Erickson had won the bid for the Montlake job.

After speeches by ex-governor McGraw, state senator Cotterill, former U.S. senator Squire, president of the Lake Washington Canal Association John Brace, Chamber representative Roger Greene, and perhaps Seattle's most famous promoter, Thomas Burke, who urged his fellow businessmen to leave no stone unturned if they hoped to reach a goal of one million people living in Seattle by 1929, McGraw pulled the throttle on a steam shovel and moved a bucketful of earth. Many in attendance then rushed down to obtain a souvenir pebble. This would be the last act on behalf of the canal for "Dig the Ditch" McGraw. He died eight months later at the age of 59, seeing only this first stage completed of his long-dreamed-for canal.

Standing next to the ex-governor, Erickson stated that he hoped to complete the canal in about four months. To do so, he would have to excavate down more than 50 feet through the high point of the Portage. The base of the canal would vary between 70 and 80 feet wide and be about 15 feet higher on the Lake Washington side than on Lake Union. Curiously, it was planned to be a dry canal for most of the year, excavated in part to unite the lakes but also to address the long-term concern about flooding in the river valleys below Lake Washington.

Erickson's cut, as it came to be called, would be a first step. It would be excavated to a point above the low water level height for Lake Washington but below the level at high water. When the lake rose, water would flow into the cut, instead of down the Black River. Otherwise the cut would not contain water. Although this sounded like a good idea, the Corps changed their minds and decided that it would be more practical to excavate a deeper cut and install a gate system to control water flow and prevent flooding down the Black, but also prevent Lake Washington from dropping to the level of Lake Union until the canal was complete. Erickson completed this project in the summer of 1910.

The new cut created several additional challenges, particularly in regard to transportation. The 23rd Avenue trolley line and other vehicles could not cross the cut. Those who wanted to reach the University of Washington campus from Montlake or Capitol Hill could go via the Latona Bridge at the other end of Portage Bay, though some students organized a rowboat ferry system to cross the new canal.

Nor did everyone like the idea of lowering Lake Washington. A group of waterfront property owners on the east side of the lake led by William L. Bilger sued the State of Washington, King County, and Erickson to stop the contractor. Bilger's lawyers argued that the new lake level would damage their properties and "that no provision has been made for paying such damages." The suit eventually led to an injunction imposed on October 22, 1910, which prevented Erickson from opening the gates and allowing water into his cut.

Houseboats in Lake Union left high and dry after washout of the Fremont Bridge in 1914.

DAM BURSTS

One of the challenges of building a dam is the possibility of failure. This has happened four times on the dams built along Seattle's ship canal: twice naturally and twice by dynamite. The first burst occurred on January 22, 1899, when someone blew up the dam built at the Portage between Lake Washington and Lake Union. The explosion took out a wing and gate at the dam on Union Bay and allowed water to flow into Lake Union. Blame immediately fell upon farmers in the White River valley. They had been agitating for years to lower the level of Lake Washington, which they blamed for flooding in the valley. No one was ever prosecuted.

Four years later, at 6:00 a.m. on October 7, 1903, the dam at Lake Union failed because heavy rain caused the lake to rise and break the wooden structure. John M. Clapp of the Corps of Engineers stated that he thought that rats probably contributed to the washout by weakening the earthen dam that held the gates. So much water escaped that it tripled the width of the canal between Lake Union and Salmon Bay. The Corps built a temporary dam by the next day. No one was hurt, though traffic on bridges across the canal was interrupted.

Dynamite was used again on October 26, 1910, to blow out the dam between Lake Washington and Lake Union. Captain Arthur Williams of the Corps ordered the explosion. This time the goal was to lower Lake Washington as part of the ongoing plan to build the ship canal, but it was deemed premature and the breach was quickly fixed.

The final burst—due again to high water—occurred on March 13, 1914, and led to the lowering of Lake Union by 8.5 feet in 24 hours. Floodwaters also washed out the Fremont Bridge, wrecked Northern Pacific train trestles, and took out several docks. Worse off were Lake Union's houseboat residents, whose homes were left tilted at odd angles after the water drained out. The *Seattle Times* interviewed C. M. Britton and William McCauslin, who lived in a houseboat on the east side of the lake. The lowered lake left them perched "almost perpendicular" to the lakebed. They also "were having considerable trouble in cooking their dinner on the kitchen range, as the food would only brown on one side." Crews built a temporary dam to stop the flow, followed by a full replacement about a month after the original dam broke. Fortunately, the flood did not damage the ongoing construction of the locks.

Top: The burst dam was big news in Seattle in 1914.

Bottom: West side of Lake Union, just above where the Fremont Bridge washed out on March 13, 1914.

Fremont Cut, 1911.

Fremont Cut excavation, 1912.

FREMONT CUT

On June 2, 1911, work began at Phinney Avenue and Ewing Street (about a block south of where Phinney now intersects North 34th Street) on the canal between Lake Union and Salmon Bay. As with so many events of this nature in Seattle, the excitement of the steam shovels was coupled with speeches, in this case nine of them. (One wonders how many people stuck around for all of them. For example, the *Seattle Times* noted that Senator Piles "dwelt at some length on the very important topic 'The Relation of the Government to Harbor Improvements in Washington.' ")

The plan called for contractor Holt & Jeffrey to excavate about 440,000 cubic yards of material, which would then be used for fill around Ballard. The new canal would be an expansion of the old Wa Chong laborers' canal, completed in 1885, and the Government Canal, which had been completed in 1902 and ran parallel to the older canal for a short distance. Holt & Jeffrey's excavation wasn't the first widening of the Government Canal.

When the dam and gate system at Lake Union burst in 1903, the floodwaters were 75 to 100 feet wide. Despite the calamity, the *Seattle Times* noted that "eminent citizens were rejoicing" because the floodwaters were doing what they had so long sought, creating a canal wide enough for boats of any size to travel between Lake Union and Salmon Bay.

Holt & Jeffrey were still at work on March 13, 1914 (financial issues appear to have delayed the project) during the second Lake Union dam burst. Although the water flooded one of the contractor's dipper dredges, it does not appear to have damaged the canal walls or slowed the work on the canal. The 1916 Corps of Engineers' annual report noted that the contractors had completed 98 percent of the work on the Fremont Cut by June 30, 1915.

A crowd watches the first work on the Fremont Cut, June 2, 1911.

1489

Cofferdam at Portage Bay end of Montlake Cut, 1913.

The injunction, however, did not apply to the U.S. government, so Captain Arthur Williams of the Corps ordered Erickson's foreman, Robert A. Carlson, to dynamite the embankment and let water into the canal, which he did at 4 p.m. on October 26. Judge John R. Mitchell, who had issued the earlier injunction, immediately issued a new injunction that included the U.S. government, and all work stopped on the canal. Mitchell also held Erickson and Carlson in contempt of court, which led to years of legal wrangling that ultimately reached the U.S. Supreme Court. The justices ruled that Williams had not had the authority to order Carlson to blow up the embankment, but by this time (May 1914) the question was moot as another contractor had further excavated Erickson's cut and developed it into the modern canal. Almost.

Work on the full cut had begun in June 1912. The Stillwell Brothers Construction Company used two steam shovels, two hydraulic giants, and a dipper dredge to excavate the cut, which would be 2,200 feet long, 100 feet wide at the bottom, and an even 36 feet deep from lake to lake. Within the cut, Stillwell built a small railroad to carry the excavated sediment east and north, where it was used for fill on shoreline owned by the University of Washington. The company also built a cofferdam, or temporary protective structure, at the cut's western end on Portage Bay, in order to keep water out of the work site. Made of pilings and dirt, it was strong enough that vehicles could cross over it. At the eastern end were control gates, which would be used to let water out of Lake Washington when it needed to be lowered.

Stillwell finished their work in late 1913, but throughout the project the contractor had problems with sliding on the south-side slope of the cut. The engineers hoped that filling the cut with water would stop the slides. On December 31, 1913, they got to test their theory when they dynamited the cofferdam and

Stillwell Brothers equipment on a barge moving through the Montlake Cut, 1917.

Building the cofferdam
for the pit where the locks
would be built, 1912.

let water fill the canal. (This was a fine development for the University of
Washington rowing crews, who took advantage of the canal for practice
within a week of the removal of the cofferdam. It was also during this
time that contractor James Stillwell noticed a young woman rowing
across Lake Union. She was Lucy Pocock, British women's sculling
champion and sister of George Pocock, who along with his son Stan, was
a renowned boatbuilder. Lucy and James married in 1917.) Unfortunately,
the slides continued, and Stillwell had to rebuild the cofferdam, pump
out the water, and cover the slide area with concrete. At the same time,
the city had Stillwell build foundation piers for a bridge across the canal.

When Stillwell finished the concrete work in November 1914,
they blasted their cofferdam a second time. The Corps was not
completely satisfied again and in March 1916 hired contractor Pearson
Construction to do new concrete work—this time to prevent slides
on the north side. Not only did the additional concrete work force
the construction of a third and final cofferdam at the west end of
the Montlake Cut, but it also delayed the opening of the locks. This
angered U.S. Congressman William Humphrey so much that he urged
the Corps' Major James B. Cavanaugh, who had taken over the Seattle
district in 1911, to ignore the problematic north side and simply open
the canal without a new revetment. Cavanaugh chose to ignore the
congressman's suggestion, and Pearson started work on the new
revetment in April.

Actual work on the locks had begun about four and a half years
earlier, in August 1911. The first task was to build a cofferdam around

the site of the locks. A month earlier, the Puget Sound Bridge and Dredging Company had won the contract to build the temporary dam. Its crew began by driving two rows of piles, 20 feet apart, with eight feet separating each of the more than 600 piles. The walls consisted of three overlapping 12-inch-wide wooden planks, bolted and nailed together to form a tongue-and-groove joint, known as Wakefield sheet piling. To add strength, three rows of six-inch-thick timbers, called waling, ran horizontally inside and outside the sheet piling.

Fine clay excavated from near the site was then dumped and tamped in the space between the sheet piling walls. Known as puddle, the impermeable clay was essential to making the cofferdam waterproof. Contractors also banked the clay on either side of the structure. An article written at the time in *Engineering Record* noted, "At high tide the bottom of the excavation was 58 ft. below water level, but no seepage difficulties were experienced." The cofferdam ran for about 2,300 feet in a giant C around the locks' site.

South of the dam was the temporary channel that had been dredged to allow water and boats to move in and out of Salmon Bay. Spaced regularly along the wall were dolphins, or clusters of piles wrapped in steel cables. These protected the cofferdam from vessels and log booms passing through the temporary waterway.

By early August 1912, the cofferdam was built. The contract had included dredging out 245,000 cubic yards of sediment from the lock pit, which had been excavated down to a solid foundation bed of "tenacious blue clay," according to *Engineering Record*. Crews then pumped all water out of the locks site and began to build a 65-foot-high wooden trestle down the center of the pit. Atop the trestle ran a train that carried supplies. One of the first items transported by the train was concrete used to build the foundations for two gantry cranes that would travel overhead. Rising 75 feet above the trestle, the steel gantries spanned the entire workspace and consisted of a frame and two support legs, which ran along two tracks, one on top of the

Within the lock pit, 1913.

LAKE WASHINGTON CANAL, WASH.
LOCKS AT NARROWS OF SALMON BAY.
UPPER END OF LARGE LOCK FROM HEAD OF
TRAMWAY.

JAN. 30, 1914.

MAKING STRONG CONCRETE

Concrete consists of sand, gravel, cement, and water. Sand and gravel are the most voluminous ingredients. For the locks, they arrived daily on barges from a quarry at Steilacoom, 45 miles south on Puget Sound (about 4 miles south of the Tacoma Narrows Bridge and now known as University Place), at what is also the location of the Chambers Bay Golf Course. Workers quarried the material from vast beds of sediment deposited during the retreat of the Puget lobe glacier at the end of the last ice age. The cement came from the town of Concrete, 24 miles east of Sedro-Woolley, and was brought to the site by Great Northern trains. It had been produced from 330-million-year-old limestone, quarried just north of town on the shores of Lake Shannon. When the materials reached the site, workers transferred them to storage bins.

Making the cement required a five-man crew to transfer the raw ingredients from elevated storage bins into one of three mixers. One man controlled the discharge lever, one measured and dumped the sand and gravel, two dumped the correct proportion of cement into a hopper, and the final crewman wheeled the cement from the warehouse.

The mixers then dumped the cement directly into one-and-a-half-yard buckets, six of which sat on a train car. (A cubic yard of concrete covers 81 square feet to a depth of four inches.) Once eight cars had been filled, the train traveled the short distance to the trestle under the gantries, each of which could pick up two buckets. Typical production was about 770 cubic yards per day, with a record of 1,140 cubic yards on one glorious day. By the end of the project, crews had poured more than 220,000 cubic yards of concrete, or about four times more than was used for the Kingdome.

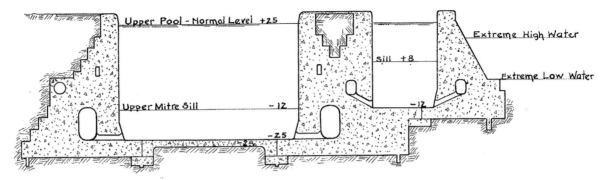

Upper Pool - Normal Level +25

Extreme High Water

Sill +8

Extreme Low Water

Upper Mitre Sill   -12   -12

-25

28

SECTION THROUGH LOCKS

cofferdam and one on the trestle. At its north end, the steel frame cantilevered 88 feet beyond the trestle.

The gantries were a key component of construction; each held two movable cars, or trolleys, able to transport five tons of supplies apiece. With the gantries, crews could easily move heavy loads, particularly concrete, to any point in the construction site. Communication between the ground crew and the gantry drivers, who sat in a shed on the south side of the crane, was by portable telephone mouthpieces, with the operators wearing headsets.

As construction continued, the site grew to a full-service industrial workplace. Workers could produce most any item needed for the locks in their carpenter and blacksmith shops using materials from extensive lumber and steel yards. They also had the raw supplies and mixers for all concrete production. In addition, the men ate in the cookhouse, slept in bunkhouses, and got paid—in coin—at the office. (The pay window still exists on the east side of the administration building's lobby.)

Concrete pouring for the locks structure began in February 1913. The first step was to build the wooden forms, which were 15 feet long and 5 feet tall, with varying widths. Two forms would be joined together and the concrete poured in a single 30-foot-long by 5-foot-thick layer, or lift. When the concrete had set—typically in about a week—the forms would be moved and put in position for the next section. A form could be reused about five times before it had to be replaced. By November 1914, most of the concrete work was complete.

The north wall of the main lock is 44 feet wide at the bottom, stair-stepping up to the top of the lock, where the wall is 8 feet thick. It is 55 feet tall. The middle wall is 33 feet wide at top and bottom, and the south side of the small lock tapers from 22 feet at

Cross-section of locks structure. Oval holes on either side of the large and small locks are the conduit holes where water passes through to fill the locks.

Opposite page:
Gantry cranes at work in the locks construction site.

The tallest doors are 55 feet high and weigh 480,000 pounds. About 4.4 million pounds of steel went into gate construction.

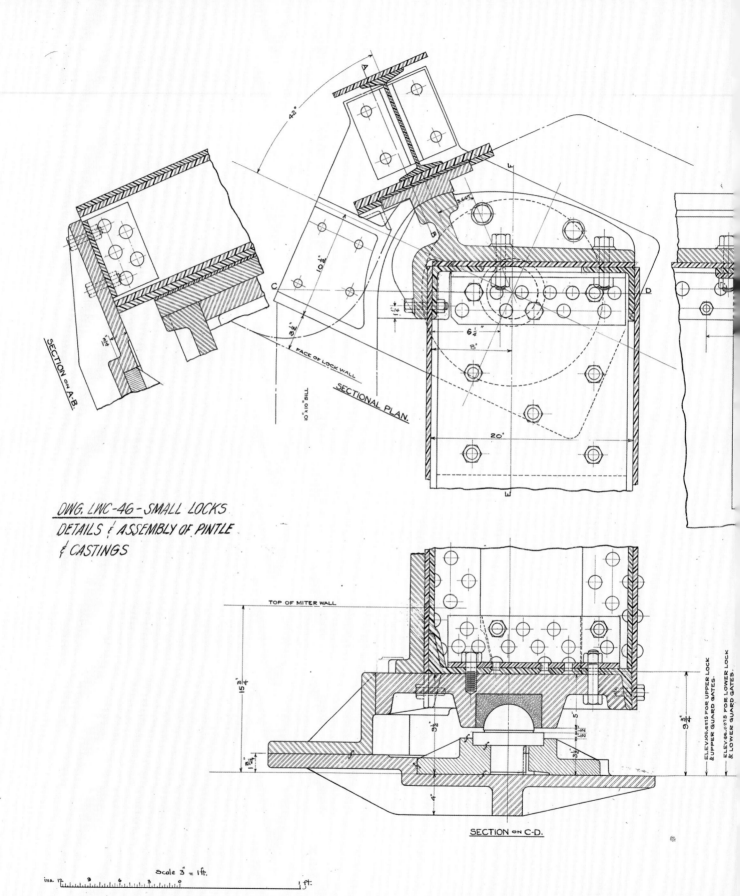

SECTION on A-B.

FACE OF LOCK WALL

SECTIONAL PLAN.

10"X10" SILL

42°

6¼"

8"

20°

DWG. LWC-46-SMALL LOCKS
DETAILS & ASSEMBLY OF PINTLE
& CASTINGS

TOP OF MITER WALL

15¾"

9¾"

ELEV.108.6875 FOR UPPER LOCK
& UPPER GUARD GATES.
ELEV.96.6875 FOR LOWER LOCK
& LOWER GUARD GATES.

SECTION on C-D.

Scale 3" = 1 ft.

ins. 12   9   6   3   0   1 ft.

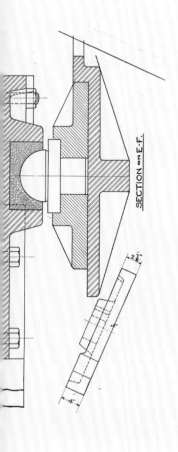

SECTION on E-F.

Construction drawings of a pintle hinge for the massive miter doors of the locks.

the bottom to 8 feet wide at the top. The bigger lock is 80 feet wide and 825 feet long, with 760 feet of usable length. It can be divided into two chambers, an eastern one that is 385 feet long and a western one that is 58 feet shorter. The small lock measures 130 feet long by 30 feet wide.

The walls are not completely solid, as two culverts run the length of each of the locks. Measuring 14 feet tall by 8 feet wide in the large lock and 6 feet by 2 feet in the smaller one, these conduits facilitate the filling of the lock chambers; water enters at the upper end, or Salmon Bay side of the culvert, and flows into the locks via drains on each side of the chamber. To control the flow of water, engineers installed Stoney gate valves within each of the large culverts. Designed by Irish engineer Francis G. M. Stoney, the massive steel doors rise and shut via a roller train in vertical grooves. Typical valves wouldn't work because water pressure creates too great a frictional resistance to slide the doors up and down.

Pintle hinge in place before lock gate was installed.

Before the concrete work was completed, workers had begun to install the gates within the locks. The locks required nine gates, three sets operating in the large lock and two in the smaller lock plus one set of guard gates located at each end of each of the locks. These would be used when the lock chambers needed to be emptied and cleaned or repaired. All of the gates were made at the Penn Bridge Company of Beaver Falls, Pennsylvania, and were assembled on site.

They are known as mitering gates, so called because the doors, or leaves, meet at an angle facing upstream and resemble a miter joint. Each leaf is hollow and consists of a series of stacked layers of steel framing surrounded by a waterproof skin, also of steel. Within each leaf are buoyancy chambers, which help relieve the weight of the doors in the water. (The idea of the air chamber had come from engineers working on the Panama Canal, who advised the Seattle engineers.) To make the leaves less flexible, the upper chambers contain water. The tallest doors are 55 feet high and weigh 480,000 pounds. About 4.4 million pounds of steel went into gate construction.

The leaves attach to the wall via vertical hinges embedded in the chamber walls and rest atop a pintle hinge cemented to the base of the chamber. Engineers in Seattle used the same type of pintle hinge used at the Panama locks. It consists of an upright metal hemisphere that fits

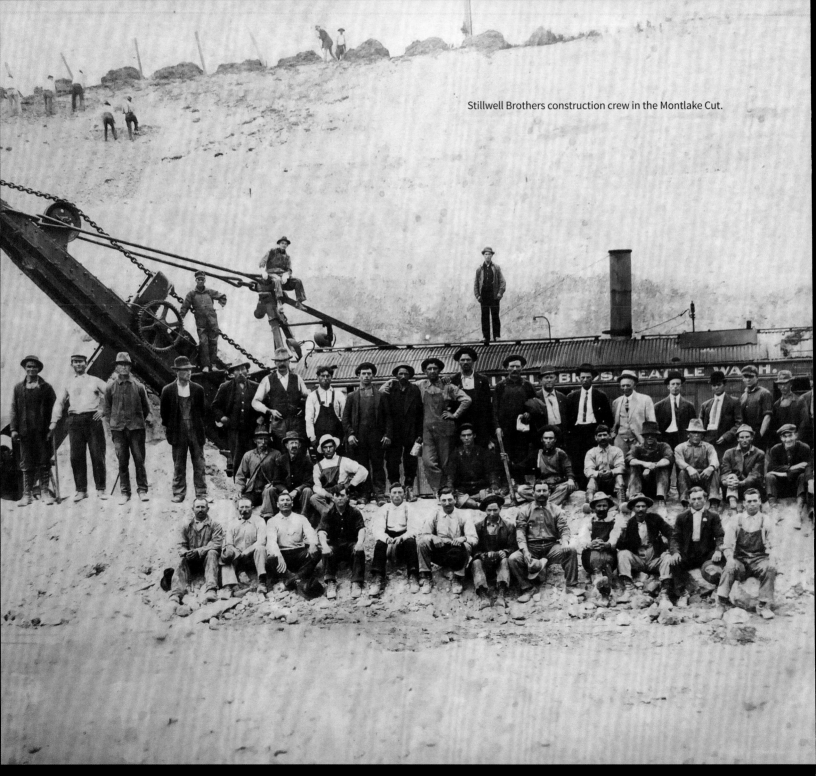

Stillwell Brothers construction crew in the Montlake Cut.

WORKERS

The locks' workforce peaked at around 350, the greatest number of which were laborers. The January 1913 monthly report, for example, noted three overseers, one clerk, one timekeeper, one handyman, one cement tester, one warehouseman, two electricians, one surveyor, one inspector, two enginemen, one cook, one blacksmith, one pipefitter, one chauffeur, one machinist, two ship caulkers, twelve carpenters, and forty to fifty laborers. Their pay ranged from $2.60/day for a handyman to $70/month for a timekeeper to $150/month for junior engineers. A typical plumber in Seattle at this time made $6/day.

Workers came from all over, including engineers who had worked on the Panama Canal. One American-born employee even complained that there were too many "forn" workers, many of whom he said were from Scandinavian countries. Once hired, workers had to swear to "support and defend the Constitution of the United States." They could be fired for coming to work intoxicated and had to worry about being suspected as members of the Industrial Workers of the World, or "Wobblies," but also had the opportunity to advance and did get raises.

We have few records beyond the basic facts, but one worker, Ernst Lidén, did leave a memoir for his family, which mentions his time at the locks. Born in Sweden in 1887, Lidén joined many young Swedes and left his home country in 1910, traveling by boat first to England, then by another ship to Canada, and finally by train to Vancouver, where he arrived in April, four months after leaving Sweden. He spoke only two words of English and knew no one except his seven fellow traveling friends from home. After working a variety of construction-related jobs around British Columbia, he ended up in Seattle in 1913, perhaps drawn by the large Scandinavian community, and rented a room in a boarding house.

Several weeks after arriving in Seattle, Lidén heard of work at the locks. When he arrived he saw a "No

Workers pour cement at the lower end of the locks, 1914.

Help Needed" sign on the office, but a visitor to the boarding house told Lidén that someone was always late or ill at the locks and that he should just show up. When he went to the job site after breakfast the next day, he was nowhere near the head of the line that formed in front of a small door. Lidén arrived the following day at 5:30 a.m., ahead of everyone else. When the door opened, a man stuck his head out and asked if Lidén could buck rivets. Although he had only a faint idea of what that meant, he said yes, and was hired.

His job was to replace bolts with red-hot rivets in half-inch steel plates. "When I [returned] to the boarding house, I was a physical wreck," he wrote in his memoir. Next, he had to pick up bolts and nuts that had fallen into the locks. The challenge was to avoid the constant rain of several-inch-long bolts that the men dropped when they put the rivets in. He later moved to sorting steel plates and beams, which was a better job until he saw his supervisor's foot get crushed in an accident.

Lidén eventually worked his way up to crew boss (increasing his pay from $3.50 to $5.00 a day), but when that work came to an end, he decided to move on. In June 1914 he caught a boat to Nome, Alaska, to seek his fortune in the gold rush.

LAKE WASHINGTON CANAL, WASH.
LOCKS AT NARROWS OF SALMON BAY.
ADMITTING WATER TO LOCK CHAMBER.
UPPER END- NORTH WALL.
FEB. 2, 1916

into a bushing, or socket, on the bottom of the leaf. Because the doors aren't anchored into the hinge, they are able to float, or move slightly, in case debris gets lodged between the walls and gate.

Electricity provided the power for all aspects of canal operation. This included spinning the reels that held the cables that controlled gate movement, electric light poles that allowed night operations, and winches that aided and controlled ships moving through the locks. In his earlier plans for the locks, Chittenden had suggested that a power plant could be added to utilize hydropower for lock operations, but he ultimately rejected the idea because the small amount of power generated hardly merited the effort. Instead, the locks relied, and still rely, on Seattle's municipal power system for inexpensive and reliable power.

Seattle's gate system is very similar to the ones used in the Panama Canal, just scaled down. The huge canal connecting the Pacific and Atlantic Oceans, which officially opened in 1914, had 92 steel gates ranging in height from 47 to 82 feet tall. The heaviest ones weighed 1,483,700 pounds each. Total steel for the Panamanian gates equaled the amount used in construction of the Empire State Building.

Similar to other grand construction projects in Seattle, such as the Denny Hill and Jackson Street regrades, the building of the locks at Ballard became a must-see sight for residents. The best spot was

a viewing platform on a bluff overlooking the site on the Ballard side. To the unnamed author of a 1913 article in *Railway and Marine News*, a Seattle-based trade publication, the construction at the locks symbolized the great future that lay ahead for the city: "[T]he work being pushed is a sight worth seeing by all those public spirited men who see in every movement of the giant crane, lift of the dredge or dumping a load of earth from the steam shovel scoop, many steps nearer to the completion of this great work which will give to the port of Seattle an additional deep fresh water harbor that will have no equal in the United States."

With the gates in place and concrete work completed, workers could now turn to the next stage of the project: connecting freshwater and salt water. Cavanaugh started the process on a cold February 2, 1916, by allowing water to flow into the larger lock. The day before, 21.5 inches of snow had fallen—still a record for Seattle in a 24-hour period—on top of nearly two feet of snow that had already accumulated. Thirty-two minutes later the big chamber was filled, the gates were opened, and the main lock became the channel for water and boats to move between Puget Sound and Salmon Bay.

The first boat to go through was the *Orcas*, a tender operated by the Corps. Within days the *May B II* passenger ferry had begun regular service between Elliott Bay and Ballard. Other boats to pass

"[T]he work being pushed is a sight worth seeing by all those public spirited men who see in every movement of the giant crane, lift of the dredge or dumping a load of earth from the steam shovel scoop, many steps nearer to the completion of this great work which will give to the port of Seattle an additional deep fresh water harbor that will have no equal in the United States."

Opposite page:

Left: The doors of the locks' gates contain buoyancy chambers, which allow them to float slightly while in place in the locks, as well as be transported, as this one is in 1936.

Right: Water filling the large lock for the first time, February 2, 1916.

JAMES BATES CAVANAUGH

Although Hiram M. Chittenden receives much of the credit for the building of the locks, he had little impact on their actual construction. Instead, credit should go to James Bates Cavanaugh, who became head of the Seattle district of the Corps in August 1911. For the next six years, he supervised all aspects of the construction of the locks, and he is arguably the man most responsible for the locks we see today.

Born in Illinois in 1869, Cavanaugh arrived in Olympia at the age of 13 with his parents. His father was an agent for the General Land Office but soon purchased the *Puget Sound Courier* and renamed it *The Partisan*. He eventually became surveyor general of Washington Territory. In 1888, James entered the U.S. Military Academy at West Point and graduated four years later at the head of his class. An article that appeared in newspapers around the country upon his graduation described him as excellent in football, modest and pleasant spoken, and with a particular aptitude for engineering.

After getting additional training in engineering, Cavanaugh worked for the Detroit District of the Army Corps of Engineers. He later commanded various engineering companies during the Spanish-American War in the Philippines before becoming the Assistant to the Chief of Engineers in Washington, D.C., from 1907 to 1911, the job he held prior to his assignment in Seattle. (Cavanaugh came to Seattle with the rank of major and was promoted to lieutenant colonel in 1915. He would later be promoted to full colonel during his World War I work but then returned to the rank of lieutenant colonel, the grade he held when he retired.)

Cavanaugh transferred on May 7, 1917, to a new job in charge of the 18th Engineers division. He was in France by August, where his company built railways, docks, and supply depots, for which he was awarded a Distinguished Service Medal. He later oversaw Corps projects on the Columbia River from 1919 to 1922. Cavanaugh died in Coronado, California, in April 1927. In 1967, the former lockkeeper's house at the locks was renamed the Cavanaugh House. It still stands within the grounds and is the official residence of the Corps' commander of the Seattle District.

James B. Cavanaugh, upon graduating from West Point, 1892.

LAKE WASHINGTON CANAL, WASH.
LOCKS AT NARROWS OF SALMON BAY.
U.S.E.D. LAUNCH 'ORCAS' RAISED TO
UPPER LEVEL - SMALL LOCK.
JULY 25, 1916.

LAUNCH "ORCAS" - TUG "WILSON" - SNAGBOAT "SK..."
(TO BE SOLD.)
FEB. 27TH 1915.

NOTABLE EARLY BOATS THROUGH THE LOCKS

Orcas – "Marking the opening of the world's greatest tidal basin, the Lake Washington Canal locks at the entrance to Salmon Bay were flooded yesterday," reported the February 3, 1916, *Seattle Times*. That same day the first boat went through. Built in 1913 at Winslow, Washington, the 70-foot-long *Orcas* was a survey and inspection launch used by the Army Corps of Engineers. It also had the honor of being the first boat to lock through the smaller lock, on July 25, 1916. The *Orcas* served the Corps until 1950, when they sold the boat to William C. Gilbert, who used it as a yacht and named it the *Sea Lark*. Later renamed the *Orcas*, the boat ended up in Alaska serving as a commercial fishing vessel. She sank in Sitka in 1999.

Swinomish – "Amid handclapping, cheers and the blowing of whistles, the United States snag steamer *Swinomish* entered the Lake Washington canal," wrote Thomas Francis Hunt in the August 4, 1916, *Seattle P-I*. The 138-foot sternwheel snagboat (often called Uncle

Sam's Toothpullers) plied waterways around Puget Sound making them safer for navigation. Equipped with a boom capable of lifting 75 tons, the *Swinomish* would ram and break snags, then extract them with the boom or a clam-shell dredging bucket. In 1929, the *Swinomish* was retired and her parts used for a new snagboat, the *W. T. Preston*, which was then rebuilt 10 years later as a steel-hulled boat with the same name. That *W. T. Preston* is now dry-berthed in Anacortes and is listed on the National Register of Historic Places.

Roosevelt – One of the largest boat parades in Seattle history was organized for the official opening of the locks and canal on July 4, 1917. Leading the flotilla of more than 200 vessels was the 184-foot *Roosevelt*. Described as the "strongest wooden vessel ever built," she was launched in 1905 to carry Robert Peary's crews to the Arctic. In 1909, Peary reached the North Pole, claiming to be the first to do so. (Historians debate whether Admiral Peary actually reached the location and whether Frederick Cook got there first.)

By the time she reached Seattle, the *Roosevelt* had been converted to a supply transport boat in the Pribilof Islands. During and immediately following World War I, the *Roosevelt* was based out of Seattle and owned by the Bureau of Fisheries. Later owners refitted her as a freighter and an oceangoing tug. Despite her pedigree, years of service in foul weather ultimately led in 1937 to her abandonment in the mud of a canal built during the French attempt to construct the Panama Canal in the 1880s.

Osprey – "To the frenzied acclamation of thousands of voices—a great roar of triumphant cheers such as Lake Washington never heard before—the new 3,250-ton wooden steamship *Osprey* raced down the ways from the Houghton plant of the Anderson Shipbuilding Corporation at 5:30 o'clock yesterday," noted the *Seattle Times* on July 4, 1918. The vessel was the first oceangoing boat built on the lake.

Built for the Oriental Navigation Company of New York, the 270-foot *Osprey* and her sister ship *Oleander* would be used for shipping on the Atlantic Ocean. Former senator Squire summed up the day's festivities saying, "Today, we behold the first fruits of the canal in this beautiful wooden ship."

Fulton – "The arrival of the *Fulton* at the Lake Union Dock Company's wharf meant the realization of the dream of Seattle pioneers who looked forward to the day when the construction of the canal would give Seattle a new fresh water harbor," reported the *Seattle Times* on March 25, 1920. Built in 1898, the 152-foot *Fulton* was the first oceangoing commercial steamship to dock in freshwater when it unloaded 500 tons of paper from British Columbia at a terminal especially built for steamships. A subsequent article reported that "interest in the terminal in shipping and trade circles verges on the extraordinary, as it is believed that its completion presages a great period of development." Unfortunately for the *Fulton*, its Seattle-based career lasted less than a decade; it now molders—looking more like a giant planter box than a boat—in a side channel of the Willapa River near Raymond, Washington.

Roosevelt leading the celebratory boat parade through the canal, July 4, 1917.

Opposite page:

Left: *Orcas* passing through the small lock.

Right: *Orcas*, *Wilson*, and *Swinomish* at the locks.

through in the first few days included the freighter *Glenn*, carrying iron knees (used to secure railroad tracks to ties), and the tug *Mary Frances*, pulling a raft of cedar logs.

Now that the locks were open, workers began to build a new cofferdam south of the locks in the temporary channel that had been excavated between Salmon Bay and Shilshole Bay. The cofferdam would enclose the area where the overflow, or spillway dam, was to be built. It would be 235 feet wide with six gates, known as Tainter gates, each of which resembles a piece of pie with the round end facing upstream. The gates operate independently and were a standard design used, and still used, on waterways across the country.

The main job of the dam was to allow excess water to flow out of Salmon Bay, which would help keep the Bay and Lake Union and Lake Washington

The first lock crew, 1917.

at an elevation of 20 to 22 feet. Workers completed the spillway in a little over three months. The lock gates remained open throughout the entire work on the spillway.

On July 12, 1916, at 6:00 a.m., when the gates of the locks closed, Salmon Bay ceased to be a tidal inlet. No longer would salt water fill the bay twice a day at high tide. No longer would the lumber mills of Ballard have to wait till the tide came in to move their logs. Although the *Seattle Times* reported that the closing of the gates was "an event fraught with vital importance to Seattle and one that probably will be a large factor in this city's future destinies," there "was no cheering, no excitement" to mark the occasion. The Corps simply closed the gates at low tide without any formal ceremony.

They also started to release water from behind a dam at the outlet of Lake Union, which began the process of turning Salmon Bay into a freshwater reservoir. Almost three weeks later, Salmon Bay was filled with enough water to allow boats to move through the locks from salt water to freshwater. Again, the first boat to do so was the *Orcas*, which locked through the smaller lock on July 25. The official opening occurred at 10:00 a.m. on August 3, when the snag steamer the *Swinomish*, accompanied by the *Orcas*, traveled through the larger lock.

A crowd of 2,500 standing on either side of the locks began cheering and clapping as the boats filled with dignitaries and

After filling the Montlake Cut, the Corps opened these gates at the east end of the cut to slowly let water out of Lake Washington and lower it nine feet.

their wives (who were not with the men, but on the *Orcas*) passed by. After dropping from the new level of Salmon Bay down to the sea level of Puget Sound, the boats exited, circled about Shilshole Bay, reentered the locks, and returned to freshwater. The two steamers then proceeded up to the Ballard Bridge before returning to the locks, where Cavanaugh, Burke, and Greene spoke of the great locks and the great future awaiting Seattle.

Within days, 150 freight and passenger boats, 30 scows, and 14 log rafts had passed through the locks. They could not yet proceed into Lake Union because of the dam at the head of the Fremont Cut. Workers had started to remove it on August 5, but boats would have to wait until it was gone before they could complete the trip to Lake Union.

Finally, on Friday, August 25, the Corps began the long-awaited "union of the waters" of Lake Union and Lake Washington, as the *Seattle P-I* dubbed the event. At 2:00 p.m., workmen with shovels opened up a small cut in the cofferdam built at the west end of the Montlake Cut. The workers then "sprang aside just in time to escape the inflow of water, which descended thirty seven feet to the bottom of the cut." The stream quickly turned into a raging torrent, causing the crowds on the cofferdam to flee the water, dirt, and huge timbers that had comprised the rapidly disintegrating cofferdam. (Apparently some people were disappointed that the dam wasn't dynamited, as had been advertised in the papers and as had occurred with the two prior dams.) In exactly 56 minutes, 45 million gallons of water from Lake Union had filled the cut, followed by a small skiff carrying a man and two boys, which motored through the opening in the cofferdam and into the cut.

Three days later, after crews had cleaned out the debris in the cut, the Corps opened gates at the eastern end of the Montlake Cut and began to lower Lake Washington. The plan was to let the water out slowly in order to not damage either houseboats around the lakes or the Fremont Cut and the locks.

Boat in Montlake Cut after the gates were opened, in August 1916.

OTHER LOCKS

The Army Corps of Engineers operates 192 sets of locks in the United States. Nearly three-quarters of them are located on rivers. The river locks aid navigation by creating a series of pools with a predictable depth free of obstacles like rapids or falls. Only a handful of locks operate on human-made canals that connect waterbodies, such as the Tennessee-Tombigbee Waterway, between those two rivers, and the Dismal Swamp Canal, between Albemarle Sound and Chesapeake Bay through Virginia and North Carolina. These locks help vessels negotiate changes in elevation between two waterbodies and along the route between them.

BREACHING OF THE MONTLAKE CUT, AUGUST 25, 1916

Lake Washington dropped two feet in the first week and four feet in the first month. After that it dropped up to two inches a day.

By late October, Lake Washington had lowered its full nine feet and was equal in elevation to Lake Union and Salmon Bay, but boats were not immediately allowed to pass through. Crews still had to remove the gates that separated Union Bay from the canal, as well as sediment and debris that had accumulated at either end of the Montlake Cut. This was soon completed, and small boats finally began to move freely between Lake Union and Lake Washington. All that remained was dredging out a 5,875-foot-long channel east through Union Bay to deep water in Lake Washington and another one west through Portage Bay to the deeper water of Lake Union, which would facilitate the hoped-for use of the canal by very large oceangoing vessels. Both of those channels would eventually be 36 feet deep and up to 175 feet wide. Work began in November but would not be completed for several years. The need for additional dredging work did not, however, delay the official opening of the locks, now scheduled for Summer 1917.

The *Seattle P-I* reported that more than half of the city's population of 360,000 gathered for the grand opening on July 4, 1917. They ringed the shores of Salmon Bay, the cuts, Lake Union, and the west side of Lake Washington. Others headed out on the water, sailing, paddling, steaming, and motoring, attending events from the locks to Leschi Park, where a great line of boats paraded by the crowds. Led by the *Roosevelt*, the flotilla traveled through the large lock into Puget Sound, then returned to Shilshole Bay, where the *Roosevelt* tied to the locks and served as an open-air stage for the speakers.

Judge Burke presided over the ceremonies, which included speeches by Cavanaugh ("The canal . . . is the greatest asset of the Northwest.") and Major Dent of the Corps; Captain Coontz of the Bremerton

Navy shipyard ("I shall not be surprised in a few years to hear the slogan: 'On with the canal to Lake Sammamish.' "); former King County prosecuting attorney James McElroy, which gives an idea of the long-term litigious nature of the enterprise; and Judge Greene, who was a key leader of the Chamber's support of the canal. Amazingly the speeches lasted just 45 minutes; although brief they were eloquent, noted the *Seattle Times*.

The *Roosevelt* then locked back through to Salmon Bay and proceeded to the Fremont Bridge for another round of speeches by more dignitaries, including state senator Dan Landon; former U.S. senator Piles ("There is nothing in beauty or grandeur that can compare with our own canal, nor can it be exceeded in utility in view of the shipyards and wharves that are destined to line the shores."); former city engineer R. H. Thomson; and former state senator Cotterill ("The Lake Washington canal is the supreme manifestation of that which has been termed the 'Seattle spirit,' which is nothing more and nothing less than a united unselfish community effort for the common good.").

Apparently, no woman made a speech or sent a telegram or at least merited a mention in the newspapers. The only note about women observed that the few who were on the *Roosevelt* were guests of the officers of the ship.

After a quick tour around Lake Union, the *Roosevelt* traveled into the Montlake Cut and through a blanket of flowers floating on the water. Finally, at 4:25 p.m. she reached Leschi Park, followed by a line of more than 200 boats that stretched back to Montlake. The *Roosevelt* then returned to Salmon Bay and the festivities were over.

In their evening edition on July 4, the *Seattle Times* summed up the views of the city:

It was a gay day of fanfare. Seattle did both itself and the canal proud. The noise and clamor and pictorial features that unceasingly marked the hours were but the outward manifestation of the tremendous significance of the occasion, a significance that every thinking person on the whole canal right-of-way realized in full—that here, completed, ready for use, actually in use, was a thing that will do more toward bringing Seattle its destined million inhabitants and undisputed Pacific Coast supremacy than any other factor the city has ever known or is likely to know in the present generation.

Opening day of the locks, July 4, 1917.

C. J. Erickson's construction equipment, 1912.

THE FULL CUT AND COST

Lake Washington Ship Canal is more than just the two well-known sections linking Lake Washington to Lake Union and Lake Union to Salmon Bay. The Army Corps of Engineers dredged four additional channels: Shilshole Bay to the locks (6,100 feet); and the locks to the head of Salmon Bay (8,300 feet), the east end of Lake Union (4,850 feet), and Union Bay (5,875 feet). Added to the two cuts, the total distance excavated was nearly six miles. The Corps completed work on the final section, a 225-foot-wide by 30- to 34-foot-deep channel out into Shilshole Bay, in 1926. But that channel was not the last work on the project. Another eight years of small supplemental dredging followed, finalized by completion of a 30-foot-deep channel between the locks and Lake Washington. In the 1935 Corps annual report, District Engineer Lieutenant Colonel H. J. Wild could finally report that "the existing project was completed in 1934 at a savings of $15,705 under the estimated cost." Total cost and expenditures of United States funds was $3,649,496.73. Washington State had spent $246,567.07 and King County $742,070.51. Total sediment moved for the project was 2.2 million cubic yards.

BRIDGES OF THE WATERWAY

1 Great Northern Railroad Bridge (aka Bridge #4)
Opened in 1914, it replaced the lower Great Northern bridge formerly at 14th Avenue.

2 Ballard Bridge
Opened on December 16, 1917, it was a steel bascule bridge with wooden approaches. It reopened in 1940 with much stronger pilings.

3 Northern Pacific Railroad Bridge/Seattle and Montana RR Bridge
The Sanborn Fire Insurance map of 1905 shows two wooden railroad trestles crossing Salmon Bay just west of a bridge at 14th Avenue, or Railroad Avenue, as it was then called. By 1905, the S&M RR bridge was owned by the Great Northern Railway.

4 14th Avenue Bridge
At least two bridges have crossed over Salmon Bay at this point. The first, made from split logs with smooth faces, was built in 1892 and rose and lowered with the tide. It survived until it rotted and was replaced by a more substantial bridge, which lasted until 1917.

5 Northern Pacific Bridge
A steel Strauss bascule bridge was completed in 1914 to War Department specifications. It was taken down by dynamite on December 10, 1976.

6 Ross Bridge (aka Ross Wagon Bridge)
This small wooden bridge was built sometime before 1903, when it was damaged in a flood. Unclear when it was removed, but it shows up on a 1912 map.

7 Seattle Lake Shore and Eastern Railroad Bridge/Trestles
Built sometime between 1887 and 1890 to cross the cut excavated by Wa Chong's crews, the bridge was still in place in 1912 but was gone by the time the canal opened.

8 **Fremont Bridge**
Three bridges have crossed this location. The first, built in 1892, provided access for pedestrians, streetcars, and horse-drawn vehicles. It was upgraded in 1901 and destroyed 10 years later. A second, temporary bridge crossed the cut from 1912 to 1915. The present bridge opened on June 15, 1917. It is the lowest and most frequently opened of the four bascule bridges across the canal.

9 **Stone Way Bridge**
Opened in 1911 as a wood trestle bridge for $60,000, it closed in 1917, when it was replaced by the Fremont Bridge.

10 **Latona (aka Sixth Avenue or Brooklyn Bridge)**
Originally built by David Denny in 1891 for his streetcar trolley, the bridge was widened in 1902 for pedestrians and vehicles, and later replaced by the University Bridge. It was located directly below where the I-5 bridge now spans the canal.

11 **University Bridge (aka Eastlake Avenue or Tenth Avenue North Bridge)**
When opened in 1919, the bridge and trestles were made of wood, which often caught fire. It was remodeled in 1932-33 with two additional lanes, steel and concrete trestles, and a steel mesh deck.

12 **Montlake Bridge**
It took three elections to approve bond funding for the bridge, which finally opened in 1925. In the early 1920s, temporary pontoon bridges were placed in the cut to provide access to Husky football games.

And here, upon the bosom of this lake, where the navies of the world may ride in safety, the predictions of the pioneers have been fulfilled, for here at last we witness with the pioneers the birth of a great ocean-going steamship, the launching of which is one of the epochal events in all our history.

– SAMUEL H. PILES, REMARKING ON THE LAUNCH OF THE *OSPREY*, *SEATTLE TIMES*, JULY 3, 1918

Ballard Locks and
Salmon Bay, 1917.

CHAPTER 5

Changing Shoreline, Changing Region

By the time of the grand opening in July 1917, the locks had already proved to be a great triumph for the city. More than 16,000 vessels had locked through since the unofficial opening in August 1916. The first cargo passed through the locks in October 1916. It was coal from Nanaimo, British Columbia. Other boats carried, pulled, and pushed through 257,664 tons of logs (coming into the lakes from logging camps around Puget Sound), 34,621 tons of finished lumber (back out to salt water), and 39,486 tons of sand and gravel (brought in to supply cement plant operations on Lake Union). Other cargo, such as oil, hay, salt, oats, coal, bricks and tile, and structural steel, added another 38,050 tons of goods.

The new transportation route led to big changes at both Lake Union and Salmon Bay. Boatbuilders, boat repair and machine shops, William Boeing's first seaplane factory, sawmills, shingle mills, and houseboats jostled for room along the shore. On the lake were boats

of all sizes from halibut schooners, to tugs towing log rafts and barges of sand and gravel, to steamships.

In Salmon Bay, the pre-canal industries of sawmills and shingle mills continued to dominate the north shore. The south shore, however, proved difficult to fill behind the bulkhead because of the qualities of the dredge materials used, and its development slowed for a time. The Port of Seattle's Fishermen's Terminal attracted new tenants into its "snug harbor." In 1916, the first large cod-fishing schooners, *Azalea* and *Wawona*, joined the 196 other fishing vessels already at the terminal; others would soon arrive. In addition, the *Seattle Times* reported that the North Pacific Sea Products Company (also known as the American Pacific Whaling Company) would be mooring its four whalers at Salmon Bay. After three winters, the whalers moved to Meydenbauer Bay, which was closer to the Lake Washington Shipyards at Kirkland. For the next two decades the whaling fleet would spend the winter in freshwater and get overhauled and provisioned each spring for the whaling season in the North Pacific.

Although building the ship canal was part of Seattle's overall strategy to take advantage of the opportunities provided by the anticipated opening of the Panama Canal, it was the outbreak of World War I, and the American entrance into the war, more than the new shorter route across Panama that propelled the expansion of industry along the canal and in the lakes. A number of shipbuilders on the lakes won contracts to supply vessels for the war effort. The Seattle Lifeboat Company (Lake Union's first "war baby") built numerous lifeboats and life rafts for larger ships. Meacham & Babcock produced the first Ferris-type vessel (a wooden cargo steamship designed specifically for the war effort) built in Seattle just a year after they opened for business on Salmon Bay. The *Boulton* launched on May 18, 1918, with nine additional Ferris-type vessels to follow. At Kirkland, the Anderson Shipbuilding Corporation got a boost when it signed contracts for four oceangoing vessels, including the first one launched on Lake Washington, the *Osprey* (soon renamed the *General Pau*). Historian Lorraine

McConaghy has written in her history of the shipyards at Kirkland that the canal made it possible for the firm to shift from smaller ships, which could be floated out to the sea via the Black River only when it ran high, to larger oceangoing ships and to move them to sea with ease.

An unexpected benefit of the shipbuilding industry was the development of "one of the best boat market centers in the Northwest." Because so many boats were moored in marinas and at floats adjacent to the numerous boatbuilding and boat repair businesses, the buying and selling of boats turned into a thriving business on Lake Union. A *Seattle Times* reporter enthused in 1920, "The appearance of all these vessels in the lake was expected, but no one predicted that the inland body of water would develop into a great selling and buying market for everything that floats in the line of pleasure craft, fishing vessels and other boats of small or medium size. Yet the development of the market has been one of the striking features of the lake's activities since the government canal was completed."

A number of tug and towboat companies also located on Lake Union and Salmon Bay in the canal's early years. Foss Tug out of Tacoma bought a share in the Rouse Towboat Company in 1918, establishing their long-term tenancy in the Seattle harbor. They later established their headquarters on the south shore of the ship canal. Three other companies also began to dedicate tugs to canal work. Consistently in the 1920s and 1930s, several thousand barges locked through annually, along with hundreds of log rafts. The barges carried a variety of bulk goods, including raw materials for cement and asphalt plants on the lakes.

In 1920, the city celebrated the arrival of the first oceangoing ship, the *Fulton*, at the Lake Union Dock Company wharf on

Anderson Shipbuilding Corporation built the first ocean-going ships on Lake Washington. Later, Lake Washington Shipyards operated at the site and employed 8,000 during World War II.

Opposite page:

Left: One of four original operating houses for the lock gates. These were superseded in 1970 by a centralized control tower.

Right: North Pacific Sea Products whaling vessels—known as killer boats—moored in Meydenbauer Bay, circa 1920.

Fishermen's Headquarters (later Fishermen's Terminal) dedication, January 10, 1914.

FISHERMEN'S TERMINAL

When the Port of Seattle was formed in 1911, the commissioners, one of whom was recently retired Hiram Chittenden, set to work developing a comprehensive plan for port facilities. Miller Freeman, a publisher who founded *Pacific Fisherman* magazine and was deeply involved in fisheries issues, suggested that the port include a "snug harbor" for fishing vessels on Salmon Bay. At the time, fishing vessels did not have a home port on Puget Sound and they laid up for the off-season wherever they could find moorage space. Proximity to the city offered access to transportation infrastructure, labor, and supplies

plus a centralized location would allow boat owners to share resources and save costs. In addition, Seattle would benefit because the fishermen would spend money for repairs, maintenance, and supplies in town before heading north to the Alaska fisheries.

The port commissioners agreed wholeheartedly with Freeman's suggestion and made plans for a terminal on Salmon Bay, which offered the additional benefit of freshwater moorage once the locks were built, decreasing maintenance costs and helping to prolong the life of the wooden fishing vessels. The commissioners also saw the terminal as an opportunity to build support for the ship canal project, arguing in their 1912 annual report, "Its early improvement is of especial importance as tending to allay misgivings on the part of lumber manufacturers on the bay as to the effect of the Lake Washington Canal work upon their business. With the certainty of a deep-sea dock at their very doors and a commodious channel leading out to the Sound, it would seem that the most incredulous must be convinced of the great possibilities in store for this section of the city."

The commissioners intended to build a wharf and cargo facilities for oceangoing ships on the west side of the terminal to serve trade and to supply Fort Lawton, located just to the west in Magnolia.

In 1913 the port bought land from Oregon-Washington Railroad and Navigation Company and traded port-owned land on Smith Cove with the Great Northern Railway for additional land on Salmon Bay, bringing the total area to 45 acres. The cost of land on the bay was 10 percent of the cost for shoreline parcels on the Duwamish Waterway, which was being developed concurrently with the Lake Washington Ship Canal and would soon fill with piers serving various industries.

Fishermen's Terminal was dedicated on January 10, 1914. It offered moorings, a two-story warehouse for nets and fishermen's gear, 24 storage rooms, offices, a locker room, a fishermen's headquarters, marine ways (a type of drydock), and marine railroads to move vessels from the water to the ways. A large wharf on the west side of the terminal was built for cargo but only used as overflow holding area for Smith Cove terminals. Before the locks were completed and Salmon Bay raised, the terminal was reached by a channel dug through the tideflats to a dredged basin surrounding the moorage floats.

At the dedication ceremony, Frank J. Hemen read a statement by Port Commission president Chittenden that said the purpose of the terminal was to "organize and solidify the scattered fishing industry of the Northwest, to provide a home for the extensive

Fishermen laying out their nets along the Fishermen's Terminal pier, 1936.

fishing fleet, to give such aid as the port rightfully may in protecting the fisherman in marketing his hard-earned product."

But the fishermen did not necessarily agree with all of the port commission's plans. When the port began planning to develop the cargo-handling facilities on the west side of the terminal, they objected. The fishermen argued that the pier and the ships using it would encroach on fishing vessels' area. Instead, the port leased the land to Meacham & Babcock Shipbuilding, which would build ships for the war effort and later for commercial shippers. On the east side of the terminal, a group of fishing vessel owners frustrated by a lack of capacity at area shipyards formed the Fishing Vessel Owners Marine Ways in 1919. The company continues to operate today.

Fishermen's Terminal with additional moorages and a new western seawall, circa 1950s.

With the growth in the North Pacific fisheries, Fishermen's Terminal expanded in 1952 with more moorage space (now up to 1,000 vessels). The port also acquired 20 more acres along the west side of the terminal and constructed a seawall to shore up land and provide additional space for onshore operations and storage.

The fishing industry and Fishermen's Terminal hummed along until the 1990s, when industry changes translated to fewer small fishing boats and more slip vacancies at the terminal. By 2001, the vacancy rate was at 31 percent, which led to the port commission allowing pleasure boats at the terminal in early 2002. Since then, pleasure boats have moored alongside fishing boats, with the proviso that fishing vessels have priority and commercial uses are the primary purpose of the terminal. Despite predictions that this policy would lead to the displacement of small fishing vessels, they remain the majority of vessels moored at the terminal.

Westlake Avenue. In hindsight, it is somewhat surprising how few oceangoing vessels would ever carry freight into the canal. Canal boosters had envisioned Lake Union and Lake Washington as extensions of Elliott Bay. But few transit sheds were built to hold cargo being transferred to and from railroads. Although the Port of Seattle planned a large wharf and storage facilities for the west end of Fishermen's Terminal, it never came to fruition. Instead, the majority of the vessels that operated on the lakes were smaller and midsize boats carrying freight around Puget Sound or along the West Coast. Foreign vessels remained relatively few. Most oceangoing freight was carried out of the lakes to Alaska on smaller ships or barges. Companies like Coastal Transportation, Western Pioneer, and Northland Marine Lines supplied Alaskan towns and industries for decades.

The ships were almost all motor vessels, with internal-combustion engines. Steamers continued to operate on the canal until the early 1950s; they locked through about 100 times

annually. Sailboats persisted in small numbers, many of them likely fishing boats, until the late 1940s. Nearly all of the vessels in the canal drafted less than 22 feet.

But not all of the post-canal change was positive for businesses. Several concerns were left high and dry by the lowering of the lake. One of the first was the Hewitt-Lea Lumber Company mill on Mercer Slough, which closed because it could no longer ship wood. (More about them in the next chapter.)

The Captain Burrows Summer and Winter Pleasure Resort, located at the lake's outlet to the Black River, was left standing in the soggy marshland mostly drained by the lowering of the lake. Burrows' wife would later reminisce about how the willows grew into a thicket surrounding the resort's building. A few miles north of Burrows, a dock owner in Rainier Beach stopped bringing in scows of coal once the canal opened because the dock no longer reached out to deep-enough water and, apparently, it wasn't worth rebuilding to continue his coal-delivery service.

Captain Burrows' resort was one of several businesses around Lake Washington affected by the lowering of the lake.

Tugs *Foss No. 16, Winona,* and *Rouse* pull a raft of logs through the large lock, 1923. By the time the locks opened in 1916, most of the timber along Lake Washington had been cut, so logs primarily moved eastward through the locks to mills on the lakes.

Then there were the ideas that never came to fruition. James Moore's steel mill investors, who spurred his failed attempt to build the locks in 1906, were the last to propose large-scale industry on Lake Washington's shores. As Lucile McDonald, author of a 20-part history of Lake Washington for the *Seattle Times*, wrote, "The hoped-for day when coal smoke would belch from hundreds of smokestacks south of the present East Channel Bridge never arrived."

In 1917, the Rainier Valley Commercial Club led an effort to establish a commercial waterway district at Columbia City. Their plans included dredging a navigable waterway into Wetmore Slough and filling around it, to provide space for industrial development. The project never gained momentum and its fate was sealed in 1937, when the city filled the entrance to the slough to build a roadbed for Lake Washington Boulevard and replace an aging bridge.

A comparison of the vision for Lake Washington and its reality in the 1910s and 1920s is stark. When McGilvra scoffed at the idea of a park boulevard along the lake in 1901, he believed it would be an obstacle to burgeoning industry that would fill the shoreline. But between the time the canal was envisioned and when it opened, King County became less reliant on waterways for moving freight and people. Railroads dominated inland transportation, and the tracks skirted the northern and southern ends of the lake. Natural-resource extraction in particular had become less dependent on water. The Eastside's coal mines, which had once used scows for transportation, now relied on freight cars. Little timber remained, and logs were generally brought in from Puget Sound to mills on Salmon Bay and Lake Union. And with the straightening of the Duwamish River and the filling of the Duwamish tidelands/tideflats, newly created land relieved demand for space that had made Lake Washington's shoreline look so appealing.

A comparison of the vision for Lake Washington and its reality in the 1910s and 1920s is stark. When McGilvra scoffed at the idea of a park boulevard along the lake in 1901, he believed it would be an obstacle to burgeoning industry that would fill the shoreline. But between the time the canal was envisioned and when it opened, King County became less reliant on waterways for moving freight and people.

Opposite page:

Top: Built in 1912 to carry travelers on Lake Washington Boulevard across the outlet of Wetmore Slough, this bridge remained in place until 1937, when the shoreline was filled and the boulevard rebuilt on solid ground.

Bottom: In preparation for rising waters in Salmon Bay, a bulkhead was constructed along the northern shore to the east of the Ballard Bridge and the former tideland filled to create space for streets and buildings.

Submarine USS *Tilefish* in the large lock, circa 1950s.

MILITARY INSTALLATIONS

Given the emphasis that early canal boosters placed on the military benefits afforded by access to the lakes from the sound, the actual use of the waterway by military installations was surprisingly small. One of the first military establishments was the Sand Point Naval Air Station. Opened in 1920 and primarily an aviation facility, it relied on water and rail access for moving supplies and other cargo in and out of the base. (In a similar situation, Boeing opened its plant in Renton, in part because it could move cargo by water.)

More directly tied to the new waterway was the Lighthouse Depot for the Seventeenth District of the Lighthouse Service, which began operations on Salmon Bay in 1930. The lighthouse tenders *Heather* and *Rose* delivered supplies and mail to lighthouses along the coast and brought in buoys for repair and maintenance. The lighthouses for the Sixteenth District (Alaska) also picked up supplies from the Seattle depot. In 1940, after the Coast Guard took over the Lighthouse Service, the Salmon Bay base became a Coast Guard depot and was enlarged to handle repairs of picket and patrol boats, in addition to the lighthouse tenders.

World War II also saw the opening of the U.S. Naval Reserve Armory at the former location of the Western Mill at the south end of Lake Union. At the peak of the war, the armory consisted of 25 buildings and played an important role in training Navy Reservists. After the war, the armory continued to support Navy operations through the Vietnam War. The *Eagle 57,* a patrol boat, the destroyer escort *Whitehurst*, the submarine USS *Bowfin*, and other patrol craft and minesweepers were homeported at Lake Union over several decades. The armory was closed in 1998. Its present occupant, the Museum of History and Industry, took over the space, renovated it, and opened in 2012.

In addition to the Olmsted parks, many trail and park additions along Lake Washington resulted from Seattle Garden Club and Seattle Department of Parks and Recreation projects beginning in the 1960s.

PARKS ALONG LAKE WASHINGTON IN SEATTLE

Lowering Lake Washington had an extensive and very visible impact on Seattle's park system. John Charles Olmsted, a landscape architect in the Olmsted Brothers firm, had come to Seattle in 1903 to design a park system, which consisted of neighborhood parks and a number of larger parks distributed around the city. He also planned a string of boulevards to link the parks together in a semicircular ring around the downtown core. One of these, Lake Washington Boulevard, ran along the lakeshore for much of its length between Lakeview Park in the north and Seward Park in the south.

Olmsted advised the Parks Department that they should work with the state to acquire the shorelands along the parks and boulevards on Lake Washington. They did so, and in February 1907, the legislature passed a bill granting Seattle all shorelands adjacent to city park land. With the addition of donations by private landowners, the public gained a generous strip of green space and public access along much of the lakeshore south of Montlake and north of Seward Park when the lake was lowered in 1916.

By 1917, Lake Washington was too far away from the center of the city to be part of the manufacturing boom, and residential development had become extensive enough to block the start of a new nucleus of activity. Ferry service across the lake supported those residential developments, making it possible to live on the east side and work in Seattle. There were several significant industries—the Anderson Shipbuilding Corporation (later Lake Washington Shipyards) at Kirkland; the Republic Creosote Company tar refinery at Port Quendall, between Renton and Bellevue; the Barbee Mill at Bryn Mawr (later moved to Kennydale); and a sawmill at Kenmore. But they remained largely isolated in the years after the canal opened. Instead, small farms dominated the Eastside's economy until the opening of the Lake Washington Floating Bridge in 1940.

The growing number of automobiles and improvement and extension of roads and the floating bridge across the lake, however, were the main reason that industry did not develop as canal proponents hoped. During World War II an influx of people took advantage of the new transportation routes and jump-started suburban growth. As with the earlier subdivisions on the west side of the lake in Seattle, once residential neighborhoods dominated the shoreline, manufacturing was boxed in and eventually pushed out.

These changes in how people used the land were also reflected in how they used the water. A new type of vessel was growing in popularity and showing up more frequently in the canal—the pleasure boat. Often made locally, these boats included Lake Union Dreamboats made by the N. J. Blanchard Boat Company and Vic Franck's Boat Company's Sea Queens, as well as racing yachts, runabouts, and launches. The opening of the new Seattle Yacht Club marina and clubhouse at the west entrance to the Montlake Cut in 1920, followed by the arrival of the Queen City

Unit 4. Pontoon A-1 in Ballard Locks. 10-13-'39.

Yacht Club across Portage Bay in 1934, encouraged the development of pleasure boating on the lakes and on Puget Sound. Even as shipping on the lakes changed, the lakes would continue to attract pleasure boats, which were more likely to be wooden, and thus benefit from the freshwater moorage, than commercial boats, which were increasingly made of steel.

As its proponents had predicted, the opening of the ship canal and locks had dramatically impacted the King County economy. On one hand was the expected, or maybe hoped for, industrial development, and on the other was the unforeseen recreational development, which would continue to grow and eventually supplant much of the industry. In the decades to come, each of these new realities would have to be addressed, primarily at the most affected location—the locks. At the same time, however, another equally significant story was taking place: the environment around the lakes and Salmon Bay was undergoing unprecedented change.

Top: A pontoon for the first Lake Washington floating bridge passing through the locks, 1939.

Bottom: N.J. Blanchard Boat Company on Lake Union, 1924.

Entrance to Salmon Bay looking west in 1915.

CHAPTER 6

Environmental Change

From an ecological perspective, the opening of the ship canal and locks was arguably the greatest human-induced change that has happened to the landscape of Seattle. Unfortunately, most of the post-1916 environmental alteration was negative. Lowering and replumbing of the lake led to the loss of habitat for fish, forced fish to adjust to new migratory routes, and ultimately made it harder for fish to survive the change from freshwater to salt water. Mammals and birds also found it more challenging to live in the new smaller, lower Lake Washington.

Salmon Bay suffered the most drastic environmental change, although years of previous industrial development had already altered its shoreline. Before 1916 the bay was a habitat of brackish water; tides that raised and lowered the water level as much as 11 feet daily; an ever-changing shoreline; plants such as bulrush, woody glasswort, seablite, and sea arrowgrass; and a host of animals including crabs, shorebirds, river otters, and perhaps a harbor seal or sea lion or two. After the locks were completed, though, the entire bay became a freshwater reservoir. (Water depth varies between seven feet under some of the wharves to 40 feet in a few places where dredging occurred; for the most part the water is between 20 and 30 feet deep.) What had been a diverse landscape rimmed by wetland habitat and defined by constant change was now a placid body of water that changed imperceptibly on a daily scale.

While not as dramatic, the ecological impacts to Lake Washington were equally as life-changing as those in Salmon Bay. Before the locks opened, a little less than 1,100 acres of wetlands dotted the shores of Lake Washington. After 1916, just 74 acres remained. (The lake's total shoreline dropped from 82 miles to 71.5 miles.) The original named wetlands were Squak Slough, at the mouth of the Sammamish River; Mercer Slough, where Interstate 90 crosses into Bellevue to the east; Dunlap Slough, at Rainier Beach; and Wetmore Slough, at modern-day Genesee Park. Not officially named but very sizable were marshes at Renton and the bog now covered by the University Village shopping center. In addition, the best pre-1916 map, a USGS map of 1904, shows numerous smaller areas with wetland vegetation, such as the heads of Juanita Bay, Yarrow Bay, Fairweather Bay, Cozy Cove, and Meydenbauer Bay.

TEREDOS IN SALMON BAY

One curious short-lived ecological change in Salmon Bay took place in the year before the opening of the locks. "Led by their trusty commander, Voracious Appetite, unnumbered battalions of the Teredinidae nation have invaded Salmon Bay," wrote a fortunately unnamed *Seattle Times* reporter. The story focused on teredos (family *Teredinidae*), or shipworms, small clams with a wormlike body that extends out of the shell. What makes them notorious is that they consume wood and leave behind a skeleton of what they ate. They have been traced back to at least 3000 BCE, when they damaged Greek and Phoenician ships. Around Puget Sound, they were infamous for destroying trestles, wharves, and vessels. Nothing worked against them except copper cladding and creosoting, though even this did not always stop the teredo battalions.

Shipworms apparently did not inhabit Salmon Bay, but then in July 1915, they appeared there, weakening trestles and docks, including one that collapsed under the weight of an engineer for the port commission. Because shipworms cannot survive in freshwater, Salmon Bay has been free of them since July 1916, when it was flooded with freshwater.

With the addition of the locks, Fishermen's Terminal in Salmon Bay became a freshwater port, making boat maintenance and upkeep less expensive.

Unfortunately, there are no contemporary documents that describe these wetlands in detail. Instead we have to rely on modern comparisons and a few passing comments in diaries and reminiscences. In addition, the names used by early residents don't necessarily provide good information, as the term *slough* implies some sort of wet area but in today's parlance is more often reserved for habitat along a river, instead of a lake. Modern ecologists would classify Lake Washington's former wetlands as swamps, bogs, and marshes.

A patchwork of two varieties of swamps—forested and shrub—ringed the lake. The forested swamps, which were dominated by western red cedar, Sitka spruce, and red alder, would have been high enough in elevation that the plants' roots were not regularly inundated when the lake rose in winter. Lower in elevation and closer to open water were the shrub swamps of willow, hardhack, and red-osier dogwood, which often grew in dense, nearly impenetrable stands. No matter what vegetation dominated, the swamps would have provided diverse habitat for insects, birds, amphibians, and fish, particularly young salmon, which used the areas as both refuge and food resource.

Early residents also told of the many small mammals that lived, and died, in the wetlands. For example, Clark Sturtevant, one of the first owners of land in the Mercer Slough, broke seven beaver dams the first time he traveled by boat to his property at the upper end of the slough. According to Lucile McDonald's series in the *Seattle Times*, Sturtevant once trapped 130 mink, four otters, and a number of muskrats in a single year. Another old Seattle resident told McDonald that he trapped 300 muskrats a year.

Above: The *City of Bothell* regularly transported people up and down Squak Slough in the early 1900s. The smokestack tipped to allow the boat to pass under low bridges across the slough.

Below: Wetmore Slough looking north toward Lake Washington after a heavy rain, 1920.

Marshy areas would have lacked the woody plants found in the swamps. Typical vegetation would have been cattails, tule, and other sedges, which Native inhabitants collected for baskets, shelters, and floor mats. Another resource found in areas of deeper water was wapato, an edible starchy tuber. Ruth Venischnick, who grew up near Renton, told of how the Native women collected the wapato. "The way they dug them, they just took off their shoes and stockings and got into the water. . . . And they would dig them with their feet and they'd float up to the top and they'd just take them and put them in their aprons, they'd throw their apron across their arm and make a kind of a sack of it and put the wapatoes in it."

With the lowering of the lake, many wetland plants suffered from what University of Washington ecologist Charles Simenstad described as the "upside down seasonal hydrology." Historically, lake level fluctuated about seven feet, rising in winter and dropping in summer. After 1916, the seasonality flipped, with high water in summer and low in winter. The Corps now controls this change because they need the additional water when boat traffic through the locks is heaviest. In addition, the Corps limits the fluctuation to two feet. A greater range would harm boat moorage and houseboats and cause problems with the floating bridges; if the water drops too low, the cables holding the bridges in place become slack.

The reversal of the historic seasonal fluctuation wreaked havoc in particular on what are known as emergent plants, such as tule and cattail. Rooted in the lake bottom, they send up leaves that extend, or emerge, out of the water. Before 1916, Lake Washington's emergent vegetation went dormant over the winter and then took advantage of the low summer lake level to grow above the water's surface. The lake's seven feet of fluctuation translated to a

Baskets and cattail mats used for temporary shelters were made from plant materials harvested in wetlands.

Below: Duwamish basket.

wide band where emergents could grow around the lake. The new hydrologic regime not only narrowed that band where emergents can grow, but it created a seasonal fluctuation unfavorable to their growth, which has led to a significant loss of tule and cattails along the lake's shorelines.

Bogs were the third type of wetland found along the lake. One existed where Ravenna Creek flowed into and spread across the shallow north end of Union Bay, about the location of University Village. Dominated by sphagnum moss lawns, or mats, that floated amid open ponds and pools, bogs would also have been primarily open habitat

with few trees (and those that did grow grew very slowly). A bog near Northgate was known to the Native people as hLooQWqeed, or "bald head," in reference to the lack of trees. Other abundant plants would have been Labrador tea, bog laurel, wild cranberry, and sundew, a small carnivorous plant.

Log rafts passed through the locks until 2004, around the time the final mill on Lake Washington closed.

Across the lake, Mercer Slough was perhaps the largest bog, or at least it had a much greater extent of peat, the partly disintegrated and decomposed remains of sphagnum moss, sedges, algae, diatoms, and bacteria. The peat was more than 50 feet deep and was dominated by sedges and microscopic plant remains. Prior to 1916, the slough consisted of solid ground, swampy areas, sections of floating plants, and a channel of open water surrounded by marsh plants. Big enough for 20-foot-wide boats to access, the channel allowed vessels to travel about two miles up the slough from the lake, to about where Interstate 405 passes under Main Street in Bellevue. During winter, when the lake level rose, water covered the entire slough and it became a bay of the lake.

But as happened with the other wetlands bordering the lake, Mercer Slough changed drastically with construction of the ship canal and locks. Deprived of water, the wetland plants would

have struggled to exist; those that survived grew in areas that could still tap into the groundwater. In addition, the navigable channel became unusable, which created not only an ecological problem but also an economic one.

In 1905, the Hewitt-Lea Lumber Company acquired property at the upper end of the slough, expanded a small mill that had been built about a decade earlier, and planned a company town that they named Wilburton. By 1916, the company had shipped more than 24,000 piles and 100 million board feet of lumber down the channel. They had also towed one million feet of logs up the slough. When the lake dropped, Hewitt-Lea sued King County for $125,000, claiming that the elimination of the channel deprived them of their business. In 1924, the county Superior Court ruled against the company, stating that the mill site was only temporary and that little timber remained for the mill to cut.

Despite the lowering of the lake, water still made Mercer Slough problematic, so crews began to drain the wetland in order to develop the area for agriculture and homes. Developer John Davis and Company ran advertisements in 1918 for "Garden and Celery Land," stating that "drainage was being perfected by ditches" on "a fine body of black muck land." One person who purchased land was Frederick Winters, who established a wholesale floral business on 10 acres. He initially focused on azaleas but soon turned to King Alfred daffodils and Dutch and Spanish irises. Although the Winters family had been successful, which allowed them to buy more land, they eventually started selling property because it was too swampy to farm, and by 1943, they no longer owned any of the former slough.

The bog at Ravenna and part of the Renton marshes also became agricultural—in particular truck farms run by Japanese-Americans—but neither area stayed agricultural. In 1922, the Renton airport opened a short distance south of the former mouth

BOATS RUN INTO SUBMERGED FOREST

On September 24, 1916, just a month after the lake began draining via the ship canal, the steamboat *Triton* hit a snag near the south end of Mercer Island. The 78-foot ferry was carrying 25 passengers when she struck the tree, which punched a hole in the vessel's hull. The captain then beached the boat and ordered everyone ashore. Within minutes she sank. No one was hurt and the *Triton* was salvaged, but it did make clear that lowering Lake Washington had created a new and unusual problem.

Located off the island's southeast corner, near the middle of Mercer Island, and offshore of Saint Edward State Park in Kirkland are three groves of submerged trees. Each grove consists of more than 100 trees. They are located at the bottom of the lake because of an earthquake 1,100 years ago on what is known as the Seattle Fault, a zone of weakness that runs from Bainbridge Island to Issaquah. Estimated to be a magnitude 7.5 quake, it generated three huge landslides that carried the groves down into the water, where they stood either upright or tilted at a 45-degree angle.

Residents had long known of the trees—geologists did not figure out their quake-induced origin until the 1980s—but they had not been a problem until the lake began to lower in August 1916. The new lake level now meant that the tops of the trees were close enough to the surface that boats could hit them. At least three did, according to an October 1916 report.

In response, the Corps of Engineers employed the snagboat *Swinomish* to remove the trees by attaching a wire cable and dragging them out by their roots. Some trees, however, were too well rooted to the bottom, so the Corps blasted the tops off with dynamite. Over a three-year period, they eliminated 186 problem trees, the biggest of which was 121 feet long. It rose to within four feet of the surface.

The trees are no longer a hazard, though they did merit public attention in the 1990s. In 1994, a salvager was caught collecting wood from the submerged forests, which due to the lack of oxygen had not decayed. Unfortunately for him the state Department of Natural Resources owns the trees, plus he damaged an underwater sewer line. Found guilty of three counts of theft and three of trafficking in stolen property, the salvager received a jail term of three and a half years.

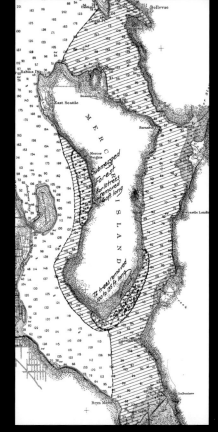

Detail from U.S. Coast and Geodetic Survey map of Lake Washington, 1910.

Snagboat *Puget* and barge in Union Bay with snagged debris.

Steel wall that can be tilted upright in the bottom of the lock, blocking the saltwater wedge.
When large deep-draft vessels enter the locks, the wall lies flat along the lock floor.

SALTWATER INCURSION

In 1917, salt water was detected in Lake Union. Prior to the opening of the locks and canal, engineers had calculated that the flow of freshwater out of the canal would be sufficient to hold salt water from Puget Sound in check; salt water, being denser, moved along the bottom of the waterway as the tide propelled it inland. When salt water was detected in Lake Union, it raised concerns that they had been mistaken.

University of Washington zoology professor E. Victor Smith was brought in to investigate the situation. He worked with the chemistry faculty and reported, "As near as can be learned, the saline intruder gave the lake the rush act at the time the Fremont dam broke two years ago, and then promptly entrenched itself on the bottom of the lake, where it has since lain, carefully hidden from public view." The strongest evidence was the fact that the waters of Salmon Bay were "as fresh as the Cedar River." A couple of months later, the *Seattle Times* relayed the conclusion that the problem appeared not to be a problem at all and fears that the lakes would become saltwater harbors had been allayed.

Saltwater incursion did become a problem in the 1960s, as the number of lockages (the operation of the locks to move vessels between Puget Sound and lake) increased. The saltwater wedge, or layer, began extending along the canal bottom as far as the Montlake Cut in the summers, when water flow through the canal was at its lowest. In December 1966, the Corps installed a barrier in the large lock to supplement the incursion prevention provided by the saltwater drain through the locks. The barrier is an 18-foot-tall wall that can be raised or lowered in the bottom of the lock, blocking the saltwater wedge.

of the Black River, and in World War II Renton's former marshes were filled and leveled to build a plant for Boeing's B-29 Superfortress production. To the north, the Ravenna truck farms gave way in 1955 to University Village.

Large tracts of the newly emerged land around Lake Washington, however, also served a more prosaic purpose. The Wetmore Slough and a cattail marsh that developed south of the Ravenna bog ended up as dumps, or what were known as sanitary landfills. Beginning in 1926 at the northeast corner of the marsh—roughly the five-way intersection at Northeast 45th Street, Northeast 45th Place, and Mary Gates Memorial Drive Northeast—the city started to dump its refuse. By the 1950s, more than 100 truckloads of garbage were being dumped every day. The industrial and household waste was so heavy that it caused the underlying peat to spread into Union Bay, which prompted the city to construct containment dikes. The dump did not close until 1966. By that time more than 200 acres had been filled with trash; the area, now known as the Union Bay Natural Area, has been undergoing restoration for the past two decades or so. Wetmore Slough suffered a similar fate, with a sanitary landfill operating from 1943 to 1967. The filled land became Genesee Park.

To a great extent the elimination of the wetlands is what the builders of the ship canal wanted. In a 1910 article, engineer Archibald Powell, who was long involved with the locks and canal, wrote, "The drainage of swamp areas will improve rather than detract from the natural beauty of the shore line." What would replace the swamps? "Excellent factory sites," noted Powell, a view seconded by many canal proponents.

The greatest post-1916 ecological change to Lake Washington though was the death of the Black River. When the lake dropped nine feet, its new surface level was below the drainage outlet for the river. Early residents described the Black as a quiet, beautiful stream. It was a good place to catch fish, particularly salmon, which used the

Top: Renton's Boeing plant built atop a former marsh at the mouth of the Black River, circa 1941. The channeled river can be seen between the plant and the airstrip.

Bottom: Bulldozer at the Montlake Landfill, now known as the Union Bay Natural Area or the Montlake Fill, 1958.

On the Black River, Washington.

river as their main migration corridor between Puget Sound and Lake Washington and the Cedar River.

Sadly, one of the few accounts we have of fish in the river is about what happened when the Black dried up. "As the water lowered slowly in the Black River, the fish sensed the change, and the big silver salmon fought their way up the river, trying to get back to Lake Washington by the thousands. We would take a big tin dishpan out to the edge of the river and dig up all the salmon we could use. One could have walked across the river on the backs of the fighting, struggling salmon, they were so numerous," wrote Dail Butler Laughery, who grew up in Renton. "It was a rare sight and one I shall never forget, nor do I ever expect to see such a sight again."

The loss of the Black River raises an important question: How did the fish that migrated up the river find their way back to Lake Washington after the opening of the locks? Unfortunately, we have no records of how it happened. Nor do we know exactly which fish species or runs used the river. The best information comes from an 1897 publication by the U.S. Commission of Fish and Fisheries. In 1896, Alvin B. Alexander, a noted fishery expert, spent several weeks examining the lake. He reported that a dense undergrowth of brush and small trees fringed the shore and that "only in a few places along the shore of the entire lake is the bottom sufficiently free from snags, fallen trees, and other material." Tule was abundant, and rocky and gravel beaches protruded from the shore regularly.

"As the water lowered slowly in the Black River, the fish sensed the change, and the big silver salmon fought their way up the river, trying to get back to Lake Washington by the thousands. We would take a big tin dishpan out to the edge of the river and dig up all the salmon we could use. One could have walked across the river on the backs of the fighting, struggling salmon, they were so numerous," wrote Dail Butler Laughery, who grew up in Renton. "It was a rare sight and one I shall never forget, nor do I ever expect to see such a sight again."

The Black River, or what was left of it, shortly after the lowering of Lake Washington in 1916.

Opposite page: Paddle trips were popular on the slow-moving, picturesque Black River.

Alexander had come to report on an 1889 release of 375,000 whitefish fry into the lake. By the time he arrived, none could be found. The main species he did find were "the cut-throat trout, Columbia River chub [modern name: peamouth], squawfish [northern pikeminnow], Columbia River sucker, a blob [unknown modern name], two or three other species of Cyprinidae, and the redfish [kokanee]." He also found sockeye and Chinook, as well as black bass (either smallmouth or largemouth bass), which were plentiful enough in Lake Union to supply the Seattle market. (In 1891, the U.S. Commission of Fish and Fisheries stocked both lakes with the non-native bass.) In addition, Alexander reported coho salmon in Lake Union and chum in "all the small creeks, lagoons, and sloughs near Duwamish and Cedar Rivers."

One curious aspect of Alexander's report and one that might provide a bit of insight into the movement of salmon is the presence of coho in Lake Union, which suggests that prior to 1916, salmon were already moving between Lake Washington and Puget Sound via Lake Union. Historically, the salmon would have been able to migrate between salt and freshwater via Ross Creek, the stream that

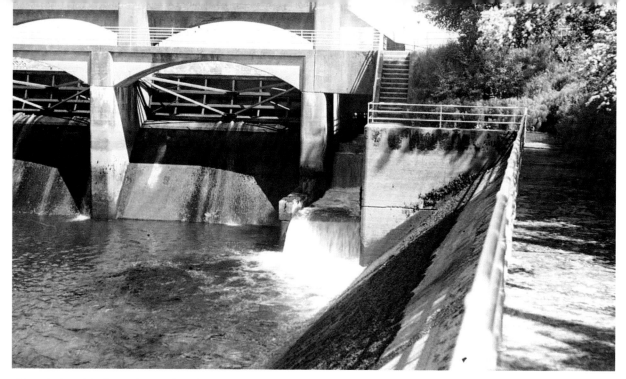

Although the original 1917 design of the fish ladder was somewhat improved in 1949, the steps remained very difficult for salmon to negotiate.

connected Lake Union and Salmon Bay. They also could have traveled through the canal built in the late 1880s as well as used a fish ladder built around 1904 at the outlet dam from Lake Union. Although flooding in November 1906 led to the removal of the ladder, fish continued to try to get to Lake Union. Newspaper articles as late as 1911 reported that people regularly caught salmon, weighing up to 28 pounds, at the base of the dam.

The fish would not have been there if they had not been born upstream. They would have had several routes into the lakes. The 1885 canal connecting Lake Washington and Lake Union had some sort of lock system, which the salmon could have exploited to move between the lakes. The salmon also could reach Lake Washington via the Black River, and their progeny could have made it to salt water through the cuts between the lakes.

If salmon were already traveling via the pre-1916 canal system, then the post-1916 route would not have been a problem for many returning salmon. Plus, when the locks opened, some salmon not old

enough to migrate must have lived in both lakes and made their one and only emigration out through the locks. They would have known only the return route to their birth stream via the locks.

A final point to consider, and like the previous ones, completely impossible to prove, is that salmon that swam out the Black and Duwamish Rivers on their outward journeys simply returned to Lake Washington via the locks. For fish that had an excellent sense of direction and ability to smell their birth stream and regularly migrated hundreds to thousands of miles, locating and traveling up the new route, which was less than 10 miles from their old route, might not have presented any problem at all.

And then the fish had to get past the locks. The intended upstream route was a fish ladder. State law from 1890 required a ladder or fishway for "any dam or other obstruction across any stream in the state which any food fish are wont to ascend." A 10-step concrete ladder with wooden weirs was included in the original design. Poorly built by modern standards, with very little design consideration for

Concept of the new fish ladder installed in 1976. Twenty-one steps and tunnels through each weir made it much easier for fish to pass through.

how fish actually use fishways, the original ladder was little used by salmon. Going out to sea was more hazardous, as no provisions were made to facilitate the passage of smolts migrating to salt water.

The locks also created additional challenges to fish passage. In particular was the loss of Salmon Bay's estuarine conditions. No longer could salmon find safe habitat in the brackish water. Nor could they find cooler water in the transition between ocean and lake. With the locks in place, there is an abrupt temperature change with relatively warm water in Salmon Bay, which leads to more predation, direct fish mortality, decreased fecundity, and higher metabolic stress. This temperature differential is less of a problem for smolts because most migrate before the summer sun warms up Salmon Bay to its maximum temperature.

With our modern mindset, it may seem surprising that the locks and canal could have been built without more safeguards for the environment. But the Army Corps of Engineers had few environmental rules and regulations that they had to follow. And as the

SMELT AND *DAPHNIA*

Not all fish that migrated in and out of Lake Washington adapted in the same manner to the post-1916 ecosystem. It appears that longfin smelt, which typically migrate, became year-round freshwater residents. This would be a significant impact on the lake.

By the 1950s, decades of sewage disposal directly into the lake had made the water unsafe, primarily because of the abundance of cyanobacteria, which thrived on the sewage nutrients. The bad water conditions led to the establishment of the Municipality of Metropolitan Seattle, or Metro, the agency charged with building and operating the wastewater treatment system. Central to the plan was to stop sewage disposal directly into the lake. With the completion of the new sewer system, the lake cleared.

Then in the late 1970s, Lake Washington became even cleaner. The reason was a population explosion of *Daphnia*, or water fleas. A filter feeder, these tiny crustaceans acted as minute vacuums by consuming vast quantities of algae. The question was why now? Biologists discovered that the *Daphnia*'s main predator, the possum shrimp, was disappearing from the lake. The reason was a population rise of longfin smelt, a major predator of the shrimp. The fish appeared to have benefited from a recent change in dredging practices along the Cedar River, which improved the smelt's breeding habitat. More smelt translated to fewer shrimp, which resulted in more *Daphnia* and better water conditions in Lake Washington.

engineer Powell implied, swamps and wetlands were ecosystems that few people liked; the best solution was to fill them in or eliminate them somehow and use the land for "good" purposes such as industry.

In contrast, modern ecologists recognize the benefits of wetlands. They buffer shorelines during storms, filter sediments from streams, absorb excess water, and provide good habitat for a host of plants and animals. The loss of the wetlands has been exacerbated by the gradual change in the rest of the shoreline around Lake Washington. The vegetation-rich, landslide-prone ecosystem is now an armored landscape of concrete bulkheads, riprap, and manicured lawns, and more than 2,700 docks (an average of 36 per mile). Another study concluded that only 5 percent of the shoreline has natural characteristics.

While these changes continue to shape the environment today, many of them have become imperceptible to residents who did not use the lakes, bay, or river before the locks. For Native people, however, addressing the impact the changes have had on their communities continues today.

Foremost among the impacts was the loss of the Black River, considered a catastrophe by the Duwamish and other tribes in the area. The river's death was one more loss to endure after more than 60 years of similarly scaled change to the landscape of the region: filling, regrading, logging, mining, and business and residential development. The loss of habitat for plants and animals created new pressures to adapt to the changing circumstances. This led to more reliance on nontraditional foods, and has made it more difficult to sustain cultural practices and cultural identities.

Duwamish family, 1900.

For generations, adults taught young people how to live along the shores of the lakes and the banks of the rivers. Women taught their daughters how to tend and harvest wapato growing in marshy areas and berries growing in patches along waterways. They taught them where to gather reeds and grasses, how to prepare them, and how to weave them into baskets, hats, and other items. Men taught their sons to fish at stations they had access to through family relations. Deep knowledge about the specific conditions and characteristics of plant materials and fish species had to be adapted to new places, if any could be found.

It was not just a matter of finding a new tule stand or a different fishing hole. A Native person's entire life history was tied to their family's place in the world. The people who lived along the waterways, the Shilshole, Duwamish, and Lake people, and others who lived in the surrounding areas, including the Muckleshoot, Snoqualmie, and Suquamish people and members of the Tulalip Tribes, held, and still hold, spiritual beliefs closely tied to places along the canal and on the lakes, even those areas such as villages, burial grounds, gathering places, and resource-collecting sites that were altered and disrupted.

They were also removed from places where they had carved out space among the new settlements. On Shilshole Bay, at the lock site, a handful of Shilshole families who had not moved out of the city were removed in order for the locks to be built. The village site of Tucked Away Inside, already encroached upon by the burgeoning town of Ballard, was dug up and partially built over by the locks.

Some of the lost access would be restored following the Boldt decision in 1974, but only after decades of advocating and legal skirmishes. That decision affirmed that the tribes in the Puget Sound region that had reserved their right to fish in their "usual and accustomed areas" in treaties had a legal right to half of the annual fish harvest. The Muckleshoot and Suquamish tribes fish at the locks today because the area surrounding them falls within their usual and accustomed areas. Additionally, members of the Muckleshoot, Duwamish, Suquamish, Snoqualmie, and Tulalip tribes continue working to reestablish their access to the waterways and shorelines so they can carry out other traditional cultural practices.

The house of Hwelchteed and Cheethluleetsa on the south side of Salmon Bay, 1898.

The dry dock *White Sands* tilted to lock through the large lock, October 1975.

CHAPTER 7

The Life of the Canal

To one side, practically at the elbow of the Queen City Company's plant, a fishing vessel and a tug loomed up in the Port Commission's marine ways, with workers clinging to their sides and climbing about their decks like huge ants, while between the ways and the boat building yards, the machine shops of Epstil & Kimball filled the air with a prosperous din. On the other side . . . a scene rich in marine color and romance met the eye—a multitude of brawny fishermen, tanned of face and deft of hand, working over their nets preparing for the salmon season. The aroma of tar filled the air. The port's big fishermen's wharf and warehouses were filled with nets and men.

– SEATTLE TIMES, JULY 11, 1917

In response to the industrial, commercial, environmental, and recreational changes that followed the opening of the locks and canal, the Corps began to make many infrastructure alterations. Some of the changes were discussed for years but not finalized. Others had been planned but not implemented. And a few evolved from a better understanding of how exactly the locks affected the physical environment, as well as with changing priorities of those who used the locks and the canal.

One change discussed during the decades of debating and planning the canal was channel depth. Chittenden's plan called for a 25-foot channel between Puget Sound and Lake Washington because that would accommodate the majority of ships being built at that time and the largest ships in service in the 1910s could be accommodated in Elliott Bay. After the canal's opening, however, some people felt that the depth, or lack thereof, limited its use. Arthur W. Sargent, assistant engineer with the Corps, wrote in 1921, "Lake Washington is in its initial development as to large terminals and industries. Owing to the absence of a suitable channel between Lake Union and Lake Washington for deep draft vessels, no deep water terminals have been constructed on Lake Washington. A dock has been constructed by private capital on the east side of the lake for the shipping of lumber by vessels for the maximum draft that can be taken into Lake Washington."

Senator Piles and the Lake Union Development Association, a group of Lake Union shoreline owners, argued that the canal had not been finished according to the expectations of the public who paid for bonds and assessments to help construct the canal. They claimed that the channel needed to be 37 feet deep and 300 feet wide to accommodate the size of ships that would be entering the canal. Congress eventually funded dredging the canal channel to 36 feet. When it was completed in 1934, the Lake Washington Ship Canal project was declared complete.

In addition to concerns about channel size, the association members felt that the volume of traffic using the locks was reaching the limits of what could be handled and they wanted a third, larger lock added. Captain Thomas Symons had anticipated the need for a third lock in 1895 and added to the canal right-of-way along the north side of the existing locks, but that extra room does not seem to have been retained by Chittenden. However, a study funded in the 1920 Rivers and Harbors Act found that "the capacity of the present locks would be vastly increased were

it not for the delays incident to the passage of rafts through these locks. This difficulty could be very largely overcome by the requirement that no rafts be permitted to be locked through, but that all log traffic be done by transporting logs on barges." That recommendation does not appear to have been heeded. Instead, a log basin was dredged in Shilshole Bay and small dolphins installed for tying up rafts waiting to transit the locks during lower-traffic times.

Despite concerns about capacity, traffic through the locks continued to increase in the early 1920s. The volume grew from 1.5 million tons of cargo and 826,887 tons of rafted logs to a pre-World War II peak of nearly 2.3 million tons of cargo and more than 1.3 million tons of rafted logs in 1923. With the onset of the Great Depression, however, the need for an additional lock became moot as canal traffic ebbed, particularly in the amount of cargo passing through the locks. In 1932, the tonnage carried in vessels dropped to 811,007 tons. It would not rebound to above 1 million tons until 1940, when the outbreak of World War II increased economic activity. Rafted tonnage dropped to about 600,000 tons annually in the 1930s.

Because the Corps based its budget calculations on the amount of cargo handled by its facilities, the managers of the locks particularly struggled with the loss of tonnage as the locks were already at a budgetary disadvantage with so many of the users not carrying freight through the locks. Thus, when the North Pacific fishing fleet came back to Fishermen's Terminal with empty holds, having left their catch with processors in Alaska or on Elliott Bay, their sizable local economic impact did not register in the Corps' statistics. Likewise, recreational boaters made use of the locks extensively, but their economic impact lay in non-cargo-based activities. They supported the local economy through moorage fees, patronage of maritime businesses, and increased tourism.

In 1936, the Seattle District tried to make a case for the cost-benefit ratio of the locks because the volume of cargo transferred in Seattle was relatively low in comparison to other locks in the country (because most of the fish was processed in the field) and operations funding was determined by tonnage handled. The local Corps office compared the operating expenses and benefits of the locks to that of the Sault Ste. Marie locks on the Great Lakes. By showing that Seattle's locks handled far more traffic at less expense per vessel, the Seattle District tried to demonstrate that the economic benefit provided by the locks was higher than the cargo statistics indicated. Corps officials do not appear to have been swayed by the argument and did not change the funding equation used to calculate the budget for locks operations. This somewhat unique circumstance relative to users, freight, and funding persists today.

As the 1930s wore on, another concern was raised. The Corps does not appear to have had a problem keeping the water level of Salmon Bay (and hence Lake Union and Lake Washington) below the 22-foot upper limit, but by 1939, the lake had dropped below its congressionally mandated lower limit of 20 feet four times. If the lake fell too far, fisheries could be affected if the mouths of spawning creeks sat above the lake level and lakeshore spawning areas dried up. In addition, some vessels would not be able to pass through the canal if the depth decreased too much, and moorages would be rendered useless if boats would lie too far below the piers.

During World War II, the barracks for Coast Guard personnel were built at the west end of the large lock.

EMERGENCY DAM

Although emergency dams were funded in 1916, the Corps would take until 1923 to finish this essential accessory element on each lock.

The original emergency dam for the large lock consisted of a wicket girder bridge, an operating bridge, six wicket girders, and 24 wickets. If the lock gates failed, the stiff-leg derrick crane located on the north lock wall would be used to install the emergency dam. First, the wicket girder bridge would be placed across the lock, followed by the placement of the operating bridge about 35 feet upstream. The crane operator would then hoist each of the wicket girders into place. The top of the wicket girder connected to a pin on the girder bridge and then connected to hoisting tackle, or cables, running from the bottom of the wicket girder to drum motors on the operating bridge. The drum motors would unwind the hoisting tackle and allow the bottom of the wicket to lower into place, resting against the concrete sill at the bottom of the lock. With the wicket girders in place, the derrick crane operator would then lift each of the wickets, or steel plates with roller-bearing wheels, onto a track on the upstream side of the wicket girders and lower them each into place. The wickets filled four rows, each of them six wickets wide. The vertical space between the wickets was filled with "needles," the relatively slender beams placed in the void between the rows of wickets to seal up the dam. When needed, the entire dam could be put in place in about four hours.

The small lock had a simpler system because it had to hold back significantly less water. Engineer Charles D. Young designed a system with five rolling steel plates that could be lowered into place in recesses in each of the lock walls.

The original emergency dam on the large lock was replaced with a more streamlined system in 1987. In place of the bridges, wicket girders, and wickets, seven bulkheads are lowered into place horizontally across the locks by the derrick crane operator. The first bulkhead is connected to a motorized hoist carriage located in the recesses of the lock wall. The carriage lowers the first

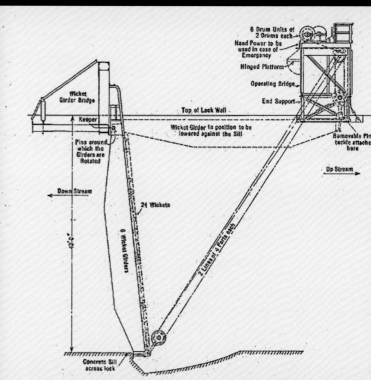

FIG. 9.—LAKE WASHINGTON SHIP CANAL EMERGENCY DAM: CROSS-SECTION OF DAM IN THE LOCK.

bulkhead as additional bulkheads are stacked on top, allowing the water to run below the bulkhead. Once all seven bulkheads are placed, they form a dam that blocks water from entering the large lock.

In addition to serving as the emergency dam, the bulkheads can be used to create an auxiliary spillway. The existing dam spillway can handle up to 18,000 cubic feet of water per second. If the lake rises above its maximum level of 22 feet due to heavy runoff or high rainfall and a more rapid spill rate is needed, some of the bulkheads can be installed to form an auxiliary spillway. As with the emergency dam installation, the water would flow under the bulkheads, its volume controlled by the number of bulkheads installed. While the spillway is in operation, all the gates of the large lock would be fully opened to protect them from the flow of water and any debris. Operating the emergency dam as an auxiliary spillway would allow an additional 22,000 cubic feet of water per second to flow out of the lakes. To date, the emergency dam has not had to be used to

Above: Emergency dam installation test, circa 1940s. The crane is operated from within the building directly behind it.

Opposite page:

Top: Original emergency dam in place in the large lock.

Bottom: Diagram of the emergency dam

OTHER WASHINGTON CANALS

DREDGE OLYMPIAN AT WORK ON THE PORT TOWNSEND END OF OAK BAY CANAL. JAN. 28-1915.

The *Oxford Dictionary of Construction, Surveying, and Civil Engineering* defines a canal as "an artificial waterway constructed for navigation, water power, or irrigation." In Washington State, as throughout the western United States, the number of miles of irrigation canals far outpaces the thousands of feet of canals built for navigation. For example, the Potholes Canal and the West Canal—both associated with the Grand Coulee Dam—are 62 miles and 82 miles long, respectively. (There is no evidence of Native people building irrigation canals in the state, in contrast to some other Native communities in arid areas.)

Washington State has only one other navigation canal besides the Lake Washington Ship Canal, but not for lack of trying. About the same time that Thomas Mercer proposed his canal, other settlers south of Seattle had an even grander vision. In 1860, former territorial governor Isaac Stevens wrote, "The country between the Columbia River and Puget Sound . . . was so favorable that it had been an idea, presented years earlier, to connect their waters by a canal." Initially, the proposal called for canals that would run from near Olympia to the Black River to the Chehalis River and out to Grays Harbor, but eventually ambitions grew and the plan called for another set of canals to link Grays Harbor to the Columbia River.

In 1933, the Washington state legislature went so far as to create a commission tasked with building the canal system. It would include a 44-mile canal from Olympia to Aberdeen, an 11-mile canal connecting Grays Harbor and Willapa Bay, and a final 5-mile canal linking the bay to the Columbia. Total excavation, depending on width and depth, ranged from 48 to 568 million cubic yards of sediment. (The Panama Canal required the excavation of 310 million cubic yards.) Twenty-eight years later, the legislature tried again to revive the idea but met with a similar lack of success.

Washington State's other navigational canal is one that few people know about or generally even notice when they drive across it. The 105-foot-wide, 15-foot-deep canal slices between Indian Island (technically not an island)

and the Quimper Peninsula. Known as either the Portage Canal or the Port Townsend Ship Canal—though an Army Corps report noted that calling it a ship canal was an overstatement—it would improve travel for tugboats towing barges and log booms and passenger-carrying steamers between Port Townsend and Seattle. As happened with many canal projects, authorization (1890) occurred long before excavation (1915). Now little used by commercial craft, or even that many recreational boats, the canal is a small remnant of an earlier era of industry on Puget Sound.

Two other canals also impacted Washington, though both were located in Oregon. In 1876, the United States Congress authorized money to begin planning for the Cascade Canal and Locks, which would facilitate passage around a dangerous section of the Columbia River 45 miles east of Portland. Work began in late 1878, but complications over land ownership, flooding, contractor issues, and challenging winters delayed the work, and the system did not open until 1896. It had one lock and a 90-foot-wide, 3,000-foot-long canal.

Almost a decade later, the Corps would move up the Columbia River and begin work on a bypass around Celilo Falls. The Corps completed the Celilo Canal and Locks in 1915, facilitating access to most of the upper reaches of the Columbia and Snake Rivers. The canal was eight miles long, 65 feet wide, and eight feet deep.

Neither the Celilo nor the Cascade locks and canal, however, would survive the ever more ambitious engineers who arrived. In 1938, water behind the Bonneville Dam flooded the Cascade bypass, and in 1957, the Celilo locks, canal, and falls disappeared under water impounded behind the Dalles Dam.

The water-level issue had long concerned engineers. When the 1891 Board of Engineers considered how much water flow the locks would require, they thought the Lake Washington drainage would be sufficient. If necessary, they thought, the Cedar River flow could be diverted to the lake. Before the locks were built, the Cedar was rerouted, so the locks were able to utilize both the lake's natural flow and that river's flow. It proved insufficient in the 1930s—the Cedar River also supplied ever-growing Seattle's water system and as that use increased, less water was available for the locks.

In 1932, John A. Fallgreen, city engineer for Auburn, Kent, Sumner, and Pacific, and Irving C. Clark, a civil engineer, proposed to dam the Green River gorge and store floodwater for summer use. It could be released into a relic Green River channel that ran along the east side of the valley to Renton, and flow into the Cedar River waterway to reach the lake. The plan could save 23,000 acres of King County land from regular flooding. In a testament to the era's faith in engineering solutions, both the Corps and U.S. Geological Survey engineers agreed to consider the proposal. It was not implemented, nor was a later proposal to reroute the Snoqualmie River to Lake Washington.

Because other sources of water for bolstering the summer water flow have not been developed, the Corps of Engineers has had to carefully monitor the lake to ensure it stays in the congressionally mandated range of 20 to 22 feet elevation. The lakes

Poster version of a sticker distributed by the Ballard Commercial Club to promote the Ballard Locks as a tourist destination.

and canal have become an integrated machine of sorts that can be manipulated for convenience, as is shown in a 1947 Corps report that explains how the lake level was lowered .8 feet "to allow property owners to repair their revetments, docks, etc." As a result of this water-level management, the canal and lakes are now a system in place to meet the transportation needs of the region, with decision-making somewhat divorced from the environmental processes and influences surrounding it.

Although the locks are part of the working waterfront, they have also been a destination for tourists and sightseers since they opened. The grounds immediately surrounding the buildings were designed by Carl F. Gould, and the Seattle Parks Department donated a number of shrubs for the planting beds. Ballard merchants promoted the locks as a destination to attract business. In 1927, the Ballard Commercial Club had stickers printed with a picture of Uncle Sam saying, "See my second largest

Formal opening of Seattle Municipal Railway's streetcar to Ballard following construction of the Ballard Bridge, January 27, 1918.

CEDAR RIVER DIVERSION

June 1, 1912, would be a "red letter day in Renton's calendar," according to an article in the *Renton Herald* of May 30. For decades, the Cedar River had regularly overflowed its banks and inundated homes and businesses in the small town. Now the river would be taken out of its winding course, which flowed directly through town into the Black River, and put in a new straight-as-an-arrow channel that carried the water directly to Lake Washington. In the words of the *Herald*'s unnamed writer, "This event marks the first step toward making Renton a commercial centre, and removes forever the menace of floods."

Hiram Chittenden appears to have been the first to make a formal proposal for channelizing the Cedar River. He recommended it in a 1907 report on how to control floods in the Duwamish and Puyallup valleys. Combined with his suggestion of lowering Lake Washington and redirecting the lake's outflow away from the Black River to the soon-to-be-built locks, Chittenden proposed that a new route of the Cedar would be key in helping to alleviate flooding in the Duwamish River.

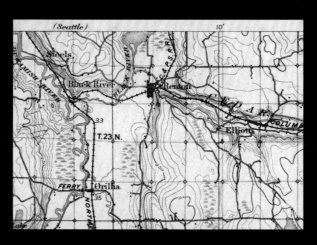

A particularly damaging flood in November 1909 provided the impetus for Renton's civic leaders to act on Chittenden's plan, though it took almost 18 months of discussions, lawsuits, and planning to obtain funding and acquisition of rights-of-way. In September 1911, the Board of County Commissioners opened bids for dredging the new channel of what was officially known as Commercial Waterway District No. 2. The winning bidder would excavate 300,000 cubic yards of sediment and build a 7,600-foot-long, 80-foot-wide, 8-foot-deep channel.

All the bids were too high, so the Board opened a second round the following February. The Board also rejected these as too costly and decided to do it themselves. They bought a dredge, hired a crew of workers, and began work. In August 1913, the Cedar River was diverted into its new channel. After the opening of the ship canal and locks, the Cedar River waterway was excavated down to the new level of Lake Washington.

One effect of the rerouting of the Cedar River was how it changed salmon migration. Before the change, some salmon were Cedar River specialists, meaning that they did not swim into Lake Washington. Instead, they would have been born in the Cedar, traveled out of it directly to the Black River, and then down to Elliott Bay via the Duwamish River. They would reverse the route for spawning. Chum, pink, and Chinook were all known to have Cedar-only runs. Chinook have been able to adapt and still inhabit the Cedar, but the chum and pink have not, and those Cedar River runs are extinct.

This 1887 U.S. Geological Survey shows the Black River running out of Lake Washington (top center) and the Cedar River joining it to flow to the Duwamish River. By 1916, the Black River would be mostly dried up and the Cedar River rechanneled to flow into Lake Washington.

Dredging the Cedar River in 1912.

locks at Ballard" and distributed 10,000 of them to area businesses to hand out to patrons. Commercial Club secretary Dwight S. Hawley told the *Seattle Times*, "We consider the locks one of the greatest tourist attractions of the Northwest. They are comparable to those at Panama itself."

Though the locks' grounds had remained open to the public during World War I, security concerns led to the closure of the grounds in June 1941. Then, the day after the attack on Pearl Harbor in December 1941, the Coast Guard leapt into action to protect the locks themselves from an attack that could incapacitate industry on the lake, interrupt essential industries and vessel movement, and do massive damage to shoreline properties. The Coast Guard stationed a boat in Shilshole Bay and another at the western entrance to the locks and required that all watercraft be cleared for entry. In February 1942, the locks were closed to all pleasure boats from sunset to sunrise. Even government vessels and others carrying cargoes for critical defense industries had to get prior approval to lock through at night.

After the war, the Corps returned to admitting visitors to the grounds and took advantage of a law passed in 1944 allowing the development of park and recreation facilities at their water resource projects. Over the next decade, the Corps purchased a sliver of land on the south side of the canal to provide public access from Magnolia into the locks, built new public restrooms, and opened the west gate on the north side to the public on weekends and holidays. The City of Seattle developed a parking lot on the north side of the locks, alongside the railroad tracks and West 54th Street, in 1950, and the Corps rebuilt the entrance gate and then installed welcoming signs and benches for visitors along the lock walls. Visitor numbers topped a million annually for the first time in 1962, during the world's fair held at Seattle Center, and the locks continue to attract more than a million visitors each year.

Many of those visitors come to see the Carl S. English Jr. Botanical Garden. English, a gardener who had worked at the locks since 1931, took over management of the grounds in 1940, and led a project to transform the landscape, beginning in 1949. Designed in the style of England's country estates, the arrangement of planting beds, lawns, and trees was inspired by nature, in contrast to the formal designs created by Gould near the buildings on the east side of the reservation. English curved paths and drives around broad expanses

Top: The Carl S. English Jr. Botanical Garden in full bloom.

Bottom: Commemorative plate produced for and sold at the 1962 World's Fair in Seattle.

of lawns dotted with large trees and thickly planted beds. He utilized some specimen plantings, but relied mostly on the effect of masses of plants arranged carefully. By the mid-1950s, the grounds had become a developed public park. Today, the gardens, renamed for English in 1974, include more than 570 species and 1,500 varieties of trees and plants, most of which are not native to the Pacific Northwest. English, and his wife Edith, who was also a renowned horticulturist, gathered seeds from around the world and started them in greenhouses located by the north entrance.

Elsewhere on the canal, the Seattle Garden Club was involved in a number of projects to beautify the shoreline. In the late 1950s, the Garden Club's ship canal committee, led by Betty Miller, worked with the Corps, Seattle Parks, and private landowners to plant a strip of trees and shrubs along each side of the Fremont Cut. The inland side of the right-of-way was still actively used by trains and cement plants and boatbuilders, but the Garden Club thought that beautifying the canal for "visiting yachtsmen and cruising tourists" would encourage them to return. The Lombardy poplar, white birch, vine maple, and flowering crabapple trees that line the canal today are the fruits of their labor.

The Garden Club continued its collaboration with the Corps and Seattle Parks Department in 1970, when trails and landscaping were added to the Montlake Cut. The Corps built a viewing platform at the south side of the entrance to the canal, and paths and planting beds were installed. The Garden Club hoped to spur development of a trail system stretching from the Washington Park Arboretum to Discovery Park via the Ballard Locks. The longest piece, the Burke-

Left: Seattle Garden Club members and Col. Richard E. McConnell, Seattle District Engineer for the Army Corps of Engineers, display a plan for Montlake Cut Nature Trail developed in collaboration with Seattle Department of Parks and Recreation in 1970.

Right: Viewing platform at east end of Montlake Cut.

Fans rim the large lock as the newly refurbished *Princess Marguerite* returns to service between Victoria, B.C., and Seattle in June 1975.

PEDESTRIAN CROSSING

One of the reasons the locks attract so many visitors is the opportunity they provide to view the boats, up close, as they move through the locks. This is the only Corps of Engineers-operated location in the country that allows open public access across the lock gates. It appears that the public could cross the locks from the time of their opening to the present, save for during World War II, when the grounds were closed to the public for security. As visitor numbers increased after the war, public amenities, such as restrooms and benches, were added, as was the fencing along the lock walls.

Gilman Trail connecting the locks to the University of Washington's Husky Stadium, would open in 1978, and the club continues its involvement in the canal's beautification today.

In addition to improving the visitor experience, the Corps had to ensure that conditions were right for salmon. The Washington State Department of Fisheries suggested in the late 1940s that the Corps redesign the fish ladder at the locks to increase passage rates. The existing fish ladder had just 10 steps to help the fish traverse an average 21 feet of rise in water level. The Corps worked with the Department of Fisheries to redesign the structure with shallower steps in 1949.

The 1976 fish ladder, with viewing room, under construction.

That structure did not improve the use of the ladder. About 90 percent of the fish continued to migrate upstream via the locks, exposing them to the stress and danger of boat hulls and propellers. The Department of Fisheries grew concerned that as much as 20 percent of the Chinook and sockeye runs were lost because of the inadequate fish ladder. Its many problems included a lack of adequate attraction water (the flow of water coming out of the ship canal), while the saltwater drain ran at too high a volume and attracted fish away from the fish ladder. The steps between the pools were still too high, and the lowest one was hard for fish to reach in low water. In 1976 the Corps rebuilt the ladder to address these problems. The renovation also included the addition of windows in a viewing room where the public could watch the fish move upstream, which has been phenomenally popular with visitors to the locks.

As the Corps worked to find a balance between transporting boats and accommodating fish, public officials worked to manage industrial, commercial, and recreational uses of the lakes. In 1950, City Engineer Ralph Finke studied the area along the north side of the Fremont Cut to determine if several streets should be vacated to make it easier for the industries located there to operate. He supported the move, arguing that there was not enough industrial

Crews at the starting line in Lake Union, 1914.

OPENING DAY AND CREW RACES

When the Seattle Yacht Club moved to its new clubhouse on Portage Bay in 1920, it brought a Seattle institution with it—the Opening Day parade, which marked, and still marks, the start of the boating season each May. It originally included yacht races and other festivities. Another long-term part of the tradition has been crew races. The University of Washington rowing crew first used the canal in January 1914, only days after work crews had connected Portage Bay and Union Bay via the Montlake Cut, but subsequent construction issues prevented regular use of the cut until final completion of the canal. In 1919, the crew team inherited the U.S. Navy's seaplane hangar at the west entrance to the Montlake Cut and began to use it as a shellhouse.

As depicted in *The Boys in the Boat* (the UW's famed 1936 Olympic team trained here), crew races in the cut were extremely popular, but by 1986, "the University of Washington realized it could do more with its Opening Day races than basically bore thousands of captive souls with an intrasquad meet. The setting was unapproached by any crew regatta in the world but the opposition for the Huskies seldom matched it or the mountains," noted the *Seattle Times*. Windermere Real Estate underwrote a competitive regatta, the Windermere Cup, the following year. The first opponents were a team from the Soviet Union. In the years since, crews from American universities and from around the world have raced the University of Washington shells in the Windermere Cup.

land in the city. To protect it, he argued that industry should be supported and things like recreational boating facilities should be discouraged along the canal.

But the 1950s was the last decade in which industrial uses and traffic dominated Lake Union, the canal, and the locks. In 1952, 2,004,884 tons of cargo locked through. Five years later, the tonnage rose to 2,700,793. At the same time, other vessels rapidly increased their use of the locks. The Corps reported that fishing vessel use had doubled while pleasure boat passages had quadrupled since 1922. On Labor Day in 1948, a record had been set for the number of lockages. Of the 646 vessels that passed through, 600 were pleasure boats. The idea for a marina outside the locks in Shilshole Bay, which had been raised before, gathered momentum as the number of pleasure boats increased. A marina would take pressure off the locks because it would provide space, then nonexistent on Puget Sound north of Seattle, for small vessels to find a harbor. In 1958, the Corps built a breakwater, and the Port of Seattle opened a marina with several hundred slips in 1960.

The ongoing increase in recreational use of the locks reflects a shift in how people viewed the region's relationship to its waterways and how decisions about land use were made. Beginning in the 1950s, and becoming more widespread in the 1960s and 1970s, uses such as parks and retail appealed to people as much as or more than the indus-

The 1950s was the last decade when commercial use dominated Lake Union, the canal, and the locks.

trial uses lining the shore. A residential development near Bellevue included canals cut into the neighborhood to provide water access from each lot. In 1963, a Seattle zoning study recommended that a new Commercial Waterfront Amenity Area zone be added to the Lake Union shoreline. At that time the proposed comprehensive plan for Seattle recommended that the entire shoreline, except for the area around Portage Bay that was residential or marina space, be zoned industrial, but this new zone would allow medium-density apartment buildings and compatible shoreline uses, such as marinas, light marine industry, boatels (steamships used as floating motels), restaurants, recreation, or park space. The proposal, although not adopted, marked the first attempt to shift the lakeshore away from industrial uses.

The relative decline of commercial traffic in the locks continued in the 1960s. By 1971, just over 10,000 commercial vessels locked through, compared to nearly 54,000 recreational vessels. Logs rafts continued to move through the locks, but in ever decreasing numbers. By this time only

a handful of wood products companies operated on the lakes, including Champion Building Products on Salmon Bay and the Barbee Mill near Renton, which would close in 1985 and about 2005, respectively. The Corps removed the log basin buoys in 2016 because they had not been used for years and posed significant maintenance issues, particularly when sea lions claimed them for sunbathing.

In the middle of the 1970s, two planning documents cemented the trend toward mixed use on the canal and lakes. The 1976 Shoreline Master Program for Seattle discouraged the development of new industrial infrastructure like railroads or adding fill to shoreline areas, but encouraged water-dependent manufacturing, cargo-handling infrastructure, and some dredging. It also codified support for the development of park spaces, public piers, and other recreational uses.

The same mix of recreational and commercial uses can be found in the Army Corps of Engineers' 1977 master plan. It laid out several goals, including preserving the locks as a facility for moving vessels

Nets being set up to protect steelhead from sea lions, which lurk in the background.

HERSCHEL, HONDO, AND STEELHEADS

Few animals in Seattle have achieved the fame and infamy of Herschel. A California sea lion who weighed between 600 and 900 pounds, he first appeared at the locks around 1980. By the middle of the decade he was famous for consuming vast quantities of steelhead at the Shilshole Bay side of the locks. Biologists were not pleased, as the voracious appetites of Herschel and his fellow pinnipeds (including Humpback and Scar and, later, Blue Eyes and Hondo, though Herschel became the generic name for most any sea lion who appeared at the locks) were decimating the steelhead run.

State wildlife agents attempted to scare off the sea lions with waterproof firecrackers the size of M-80s. The sea lions returned within hours. Agents then tried using irritating acoustic devices, providing fish that made the sea lions sick, hazing with boats, shooting rubber bullets and blunt-tipped arrows, and capturing and relocating. (A radio transmitter attached to the 1,000-pound Hondo revealed his return nine months later from California.) Some

methods initially worked, but the sea lions soon adapted to or ignored the deterrents.

Throughout the years of sea lion depredation, biologists had considered killing the animals, but the sea lions were protected by the Marine Mammal Protection Act of 1972. In addition, whenever the idea of killing arose, members of the public objected. In 1994, however, the United States Congress amended the act to allow small incidental takes of "nuisance predators." The change allowed killing to occur at the locks, but only as a last resort.

Ultimately, no one had to kill any of the sea lions. In 1996, Hondo and two other sea lions—Bob and Fred—were moved to SeaWorld in Florida. With the troublemakers moved away to a place they could not return from, the problem was resolved.

Unfortunately, only about 70 steelhead—down from peaks in the early 1980s of 2,000 to 3,000—remained. Despite the removal of sea lions, the number of steelhead has continued to remain low.

between the lakes and Puget Sound, and developing a plan to "maximize visitor enjoyment." As a result of the plan, in November 1977, the Corps' first regional visitor center opened in the 1915 carpenter/blacksmith shop, remodeled to house educational exhibits and a theater for showing films about canal history and operations.

The 1980s opened with a bang when the turnbuckles on the north leaf of the downstream gate of the small lock failed in March 1981. For three months, only the large lock operated, which was problematic because it required so much more water per lockage than the small lock. By the time the small lock was in service again, the annual summer drought had already begun, and the Corps struggled to maintain the lakes' water level over the summer. Concerns grew that the two cross-lake floating bridges would require adjustments to their cables and that salt water would encroach into Lake Washington. The situation was resolved in the early fall, when conservation efforts, increased rain, and increased releases of water from the Chester Morse Reservoir into the Cedar River raised the water level enough to halt the salt water at the Montlake Cut and protect the bridges.

The tension between recreational and industrial uses along the lake continued. In 1982, an assessment of the canal and Lake Union shoreline found that nearly 60 percent of the shoreline was occupied by water-dependent industries and businesses. Another 20 percent served water-dependent recreational uses. When city officials proposed a park for the south end of the lake, disagreements arose over the best use of the land. One 1989 city report argued that "the Ship Canal including Salmon Bay is solidly, irrevocably industrial," but then expressed concern that the Northwest Steel Rolling Mill on the canal in Ballard might close. The same discussion has played out in all of Seattle's industrial areas. Suitable land for industry is scarce, and any encroachment by

Tug with gravel barge in the large lock, 2010.

nonindustrial users threatens the viability of the industrial district.

In the 1980s and 1990s, commercial vessels remained a substantial portion of the canal's traffic. Pleasure boats outnumbered them almost 5 to 1 by the mid-1990s, but about 2 million tons of cargo passed through the locks each year. The commodities passing through—sand and gravel, oil, and still some rafted logs—relied on the waterways transport because overland transport was too inefficient and difficult in the midst of the urban area.

In the 21st century, the Corps, the Port of Seattle, and regional governments, as well as the industries, businesses, and residents of the area, have a stake in the future of the ship canal. Like other regional infrastructures, the locks are aging and there are concerns about upgrades needed to ensure that they continue to function well and to protect them from a strong earthquake. The operation of the regional transportation system relies on the integrity of the locks. If they fail, one of the largest impacts would be the effect it would have on the two floating bridges across Lake Washington. There are also concerns about the role the locks can play in supporting salmon recovery. The fish ladder improvements in 1976 helped, but the locks still pose problems for adults passing upstream and juveniles going out to the ocean.

The locks and canal continue to serve an important role in King County's economy. Fishermen's Terminal's North Pacific fishing fleet brings in about half of the American seafood catch each year. Though much of the seafood is processed at sea, the locks provide access to a freshwater, protected harbor for the fishing boats. The small vessels, many of which could not operate economically without the savings in maintenance made possible by the freshwater harbor, still rely on the economies of scale provided by vessel owners sharing resources.

The locks also provide access to the lakes for a number of economically important vessels and commodities, such as several cement plants, which supply building materials for residential and commercial construction, streets, and other infrastructure. In addition, the continued popularity of pleasure boats supports numerous boatbuilding, sales, repair, and moorage companies. And finally, the locks make it possible to move things that need to get into or out of the lakes and can go no other way, such as the 77 pontoons for the 2016 State Route 520 floating bridge replacement, the barging of houses, and even a massive drydock that barely squeaked through.

The locks also attract more than a million visitors each year and transport thousands of tourists between the lakes and Puget Sound on excursion boats. Both the Fremont and Montlake Cuts further serve local recreation and travel needs by allowing easy access between the lakes and Salmon Bay. Plus, the Montlake Cut has been home to the opening day of boating season parade and the Windermere Cup crew races for decades.

The Lake Washington Ship Canal and Hiram M. Chittenden Locks serve as a vital link in the regional transportation system, but also have played an

Top: Opening Day of boating season brings thousands of recreational boaters onto the waterway.

Bottom: A pontoon for the new SR 520 bridge over Lake Washington locking through in 2013.

Opposite page: A ship passes through the locks in 2002 during the Tall Ships Parade.

There are few places on the West Coast with as diversified a maritime economy as Seattle—from fishing to container ships to boatbuilding to pleasure boats of all kinds. In fact, it's hard to separate the waterway from the history and character of the city itself. Of the many Seattle neighborhoods that line the waterway from Shilshole to Lake Washington's Union Bay, almost all of them owe much of their individual character to their specific situation on this unique thoroughfare.

important role in shaping the character of the region. It is hard to imagine the lakes without a connection to Puget Sound. The canal has been a passage between the interior and the wider world, not a closed system. Vessels passing through bring cargo and people from around the world into the middle of the city.

The ship canal has played a role in the success of Seattle as a port city. Having access to a freshwater harbor and the development of a maritime industrial district with a distinct character strengthened the maritime economy in the region as a whole. There are few places on the West Coast with as diversified a maritime economy as Seattle—from fishing to container ships to boatbuilding to pleasure boats of all kinds. In fact, it's hard to separate the waterway from the history and character of the city itself. Of the many Seattle neighborhoods that line the waterway from Shilshole to Lake Washington's Union Bay, almost all of them owe much of their individual character to their specific situation on this unique thoroughfare.

Just as this corridor between freshwater and salt water shaped the lives of the Native people who lived here for thousands of years, it has shaped the lives of Seattleites since the grand opening of the locks and canal in 1917, and, arguably, since Thomas Mercer uttered his fateful words 63 years earlier.

MEMORIALS AT THE LOCKS

Administration Building Plaque – Designed in 1922 by Bebb and Gould, but not cast until 1985, when the Corps found the original designs for it. It honors Lieutenant Colonel James B. Cavanaugh and his assistants: Major Arthur Williams, Captain Arthur R. Ehrnbeck, Arthur W. Sargent, and Charles A. D. Young.

Carl S. English Jr. Plaque – Placed at the entrance to the botanical garden to dedicate to and name it in honor of Carl S. English Jr. in 1974. English worked as a horticulturist at the locks from 1931 to 1973, and was in charge of the grounds from 1940 until his retirement.

James B. Cavanaugh Plaque – The lockkeeper's house was renovated and made the Seattle District Commander's residence in 1974. Upon its dedication, a plaque was placed on the residence in honor of Lieutenant Colonel James B. Cavanaugh, the District Engineer who oversaw the construction of the Lake Washington Ship Canal from 1911 to 1917.

50th-Anniversary Plaque – Erected on National Maritime Day 1967 by the Yukon Club and the Port of Seattle Chapter of the Propeller Club, the plaque marks the 50th anniversary of the Chittenden Locks.

75th-Anniversary Plaque – Erected in 1992 by the Magnolia Community Club to commemorate the 75th anniversary of the opening of the locks.

Thomas Petersen Marker – Placed in 1976 during Maritime Week celebrations by the Yukon Club and the Seattle Chapter of the U.S. Propeller Club in honor of Thomas Heinrich Petersen, a shipbuilder in Ballard.

Carl English is presented with a plaque dedicated to his many years of service in 1974.

West door of the large lock during routine maintenance, 2016.

SHIP CANAL TIMELINE

July 4, 1854
Thomas Mercer proposes canal

June 12, 1861
Harvey Pike acquires land between Lake Union and Lake Washington (sometime in next few years he attempts to build a canal, with limited success)

March 1, 1864
Earliest written mention of canal, in *Seattle Gazette*, with map

January 6, 1871
Incorporation of Lake Washington Canal Company to build a canal connecting Lake Washington, Lake Union, and Puget Sound

December 13, 1871
Office of Board of Engineers for Pacific Coast submits report on canal routes between freshwater and salt water. No action taken

March 3, 1883
Incorporation of Lake Washington Improvement Company to build a canal connecting Lake Washington, Lake Union, and Puget Sound

June 7, 1883
J. J. Cummings awarded contract to cut canal

October 13, 1883
Wa Chong Company hired to replace Cummings on canal work

January 1884
Wa Chong laborers start work on canal between Salmon Bay and Lake Union

1887
At an undetermined date, laborers finish work on the canals between freshwater and salt water

September 19, 1890
U.S. Congress passes Rivers and Harbors Act of 1890, which authorizes a study of a canal between Puget Sound and Lake Sammamish

January 2, 1892
Corps of Engineers releases study of canal authorized in 1890

1893
Eugene Semple files plans to excavate a canal through Beacon Hill

March 2, 1894
U.S. Congress passes Rivers and Harbors Act, which allocates $25,000 for a study of a canal between Salmon Bay and Lake Washington

June 22, 1894
Semple establishes Seattle and Lake Washington Waterway Company to excavate canal

June 3, 1896
U.S. Congress passes Rivers and Harbors Act, which allocates $150,000 for improvements of a canal between Salmon Bay and Lake Washington

1897
Beginning of Klondike Gold Rush

April 14, 1898
Secretary of War designates Shilshole Bay as terminus of canal

Spring 1901
Excavation of Government Canal between Salmon Bay and Lake Union begins

November 1901
Semple begins work on canal through Beacon Hill

October 15, 1902
Government Canal completed

October 1903
Fremont dam bursts

June 13, 1904
Seattle City Council cuts off water supply to Semple's canal, which stops the project

December 1907
Hiram M. Chittenden releases his report for canal

October 27, 1909
C.J. Erickson begins work on Montlake Cut

February 1910
Hiram M. Chittenden retires

Summer 1910
Erickson finishes work on Montlake Cut

June 2, 1911
Holt & Jeffrey begin work on Fremont Cut

August 1911
Work begins on cofferdam at locks site

June 1, 1912
Work begins on diversion of Cedar River into Lake Washington

December 31, 1913
Union Bay cofferdam blown up, first time

January 10, 1914
Fishermen's Terminal dedicated

November 11, 1914
Union Bay cofferdam blown up, second time

February 2, 1916
First water allowed to flow into locks. First boat in locks is Corps of Engineers vessel *Orcas*

July 12, 1916
Locks closed and flooding of Salmon Bay begins

July 25, 1916
Orcas becomes first boat to travel through the smaller lock

August 3, 1916
Swinomish and *Orcas* travel through the larger lock

August 25, 1916
Union Bay cofferdam destroyed, third time

August 28, 1916
Lowering of Lake Washington begins

November/December 1916
First boats able to go from Shilshole Bay to Lake Washington

June 15, 1917
Fremont Bridge opens

July 4, 1917
Official grand opening of ship canal and locks

December 16, 1917
Ballard Bridge opens

July 1, 1919
University Bridge opens

August 1923
Emergency dam completed

June 27, 1925
Montlake Bridge opens

February 22, 1932
Aurora Bridge opens

December 29, 1934
Lake Washington Ship Canal officially complete

December 1966
Corps installs new saltwater incursion barrier

June 1, 1976
New fish ladder dedicated at locks

LAKE WASHINGTON CANAL, WASH.
LOCKS AT NARROWS OF SALMON BAY.
DISCHARGE OPENING OF CULVERTS, SOUTH
SIDE, 10' x 16' LOWER SERVICE GATE RECESS.
DEC. 11, 1913.

ACKNOWLEDGMENTS

We would like to gratefully acknowledge the many people who talked with us, shared their knowledge and expertise, read parts of our manuscript, and led us to the sources that helped us tell the story of the Lake Washington Ship Canal: Leslie Aickin, Jill Anderson (King County Archives), Skip Berger, George Blomberg (Port of Seattle), Eleanor Boba (Making the Cut), Joe Bopp (Seattle Public Library), Martha Brace, Amanda Brack (Columbia Basin Development League), Jeff Bradley (Burke Museum), Shirin Bridges, Mary Brown (City of Seattle Department of Transportation), David Buerge, Valarie Bunn (wedgwoodinseattlehistory.com), Karl Burton (Seattle Public Utilities), John Buswell (City of Seattle Department of Transportation), Judie Clarridge (Fremont Historical Society), Tim Colton (shipbuildinghistory.com), Courtney Cooper, Laura Cooper, Bethany Craig (Washington Department of Fish and Wildlife), BJ Cummings, Curtis DeGasperi (King County Water and Land Resources), Paul Dorpat, William Dowell (Army Corps of Engineers), Nancy Dulaney (Rainier Valley Historical Society), Ron Edge, Ann Ferguson (Seattle Public Library), Anne Frantilla (City of Seattle Archives), Sarah Frederick (Eastside Heritage Center), David Giblin (Burke Museum), Michael Herschensohn (Queen Anne Historical Society), Ken House (National Archives-Seattle), Anne Jenner (Special Collections, University of Washington Library), Jack Johnson (Burke Museum), Larry Johnson, Brian Kamens (Tacoma Public Library), John LaMont (Seattle Public Library), Greg Lange (King County Archives), Genevieve LeMoine (Peary-MacMillan Arctic Museum and Arctic Studies Center), Dennis Lewarch (Suquamish Tribe), Gary Lundell (Special

Collections, University of Washington Library), Michael Machette, Carolyn Marr (Museum of History and Industry), Katherine Maslenikov (Burke Museum), Nate McGowan (Army Corps of Engineers), William McLaughlin, Patty McNamee (National Archives-Seattle), Steven Mullen-Moses (Snoqualmie Tribe), Ralph Naess (Seattle Public Utilities), Assunta Ng (*Northwest Asian Weekly*), Cass O'Callaghan (Ballard Historical Society), Tom O'Grady (Friends of the Ballard Locks), Ray Owens, Laura Phillips (Burke Museum), Pat Pierce (Bothell Historical Museum), Fred Poyner IV (Nordic Heritage Museum), Tom Quinn (School of Aquatic and Fishery Sciences, University of Washington), Vaun Raymond, Tim Robinson (*Ballard News-Tribune*), Joe Rocchio (Washington Department of Natural Resources), Judie Romeo (The Center for Wooden Boats), Jim Ryan, Sarah Samson (Renton History Museum), Jack Segal, Amir Sheikh, Carol Shenk (King County Archives), Si Simenstad (School of Aquatic and Fishery Sciences, University of Washington), Richard Smith (Army Corps of Engineers), Brian Stenehjem (Army Corps of Engineers), Elizabeth Stewart (Renton History Museum), Kathy Troost (Earth and Space Sciences, University of Washington), Patrick Trotter, Matt Tyler (Jefferson County Parks and Recreation), Dick Wagner (The Center for Wooden Boats), Eric Wagner (Fisheries Biologist, Muckleshoot Tribe), Carol Whipple, William Willingham, Jonathan Wilson (Renton Airport), Jordan Wong (Wing Luke Museum), Roger Woo, Teresa Woo-Murray, Mikala Woodward (Making the Cut), Ken Yocum (Department of Landscape Architecture, University of Washington).

We'd especially like to thank Susan Connole from the Friends of the Ballard Locks. Her work gathering, organizing, and studying the documents, photos, and artifacts related to the ship canal has been invaluable in preserving and telling the stories of the people who built the locks and who have operated them for a century. She was more than generous with her time and knowledge, and we enjoyed working with her immensely. Thanks also to Katie McGillvray for a fabulous tour down the scary scaffolding into the big lock chamber.

We are grateful to everyone who helped HistoryLink pull together the funding for this book and other projects commemorating the centennial of the locks and ship canal, especially Representative Gael Tarleton, King County Councilmember Jeanne Kohl-Welles, Seattle City Councilmember Tim Burgess, Port of Seattle commissioners John Creighton and Fred Felleman, Deputy County Executive Sung Yang, Washington Sea Grant Director Penelope Dalton, and Jordan Royer, Pacific Merchant Shipping Association.

We would also like to thank Marie McCaffrey of HistoryLink for her amazing development and support of this project and Petyr Beck of Documentary Media for his editing and support and for his keeping us on target in getting this book finished. And wow, we owe so much to Judy Gouldthorpe for her exemplary copy editing, proofreading, and fact checking.

David would like to give a huge thanks to his co-author Jennifer Ott. She is an incredible researcher, always tolerant of my editing, joyfully enthusiastic about history, and a thoughtful writer. Plus her ability to laugh at some of the absurdities of co-writing has made this book a joy to work on.

Jennifer would like to send that gratitude right back to David. It has been a pleasure to see the ship canal through the eyes of a geologist-historian and to tell this story with him. David's generosity of spirit, keen intellect, and incisive writing made the back-and-forth of writing and editing a pleasure rather than a chore. Beyond the writing, it was great fun to share the thrill of obscure finds with him. She would also like to acknowledge appreciatively that this project was supported, in part, by an award from 4Culture. Finally, she'd like to thank heartfully her family, Brad, Henry, and Elliot, for sticking with her as she dove deep into the ship canal over many months.

BIBLIOGRAPHY

ARTICLES

"Construction of Lake Washington Canal Giant Undertaking." *Railway and Marine News*, September 1, 1913, pp. 22-26.

Edmonson, W. T., and Sally E. B. Abella. "Unplanned Biomanipulation in Lake Washington." *Limnologica* 19 (1), July 1988, pp. 73-79.

Erickson, A. L. "Efficient Plant for Building Locks on Ship Canal." *The Cement Era* 12 (2), February 1914, pp. 50-53.

Ficken, Robert E. "Seattle's 'Ditch': The Corps of Engineers and the Lake Washington Ship Canal." *Pacific Northwest Quarterly* 77 (1), pp. 11-20, January 1986.

Hynding, Alan A. "Eugene Semple's Seattle Canal Scheme." *Pacific Northwest Quarterly* 59 (2), April 1968, pp. 77-87.

Kidston, William L. "Connecting Lake Washington, Seattle, with Puget Sound." *Engineering Record* 66 (3), December 7, 1912, pp. 640-642.

"Lake Washington Canal." *Pacific Builder and Engineer* 13 (18), May 18, 1912, p. 18.

"Lake Washington Canal." *Pacific Builder and Engineer* 22 (4), July 28, 1916, p. 423.

McDonald, Lucile. Lake Washington history series. *The Seattle Times*, October 1955 – February 1956.

Powell, Archibald O. "The Proposed Lake Washington Canal: A Great Engineering Project." *Engineering News* 63 (1), January 6, 1910, pp. 1-5.

Rollins, C. H. "Work of the Seattle & Lake Washington Waterway Company." *Proceedings/Pacific Northwest Society of Engineers*, May 1904, pp. 1-16.

Scott, W. A. "Improvements on Lake Washington Ship Canal." *Engineering World* 19 (4), October 1921, pp. 243-244.

"200,000 Yards of Concrete Placed for $800,000 in Lake Washington Canal Lock." *Engineering Record* 72 (5), July 31, 1915, pp. 141-143.

BOOKS

Aznoff, Dan. *Renton: The First 100 Years, 1901-2001*. Renton, WA: Boeing Company, *Renton Reporter*, City of Renton, 2001.

Bagley, Clarence. *History of King County, Washington*. Chicago and Seattle: S. J. Clarke Publishing Co., 1929.

Bagley, Clarence. *History of Seattle: From the Earliest Settlement to the Present Time*. Chicago: S. J. Clarke Publishing Co., 1916.

Dodds, Gordon B. *Hiram Martin Chittenden: His Public Career*. Lexington: University Press of Kentucky, 1973.

Droker, Howard. *Seattle's Unsinkable Houseboats: An Illustrated History*. Seattle: Watermark Press, 1977.

Hynding, Alan. *The Public Life of Eugene Semple: Promoter and Politician of the Pacific Northwest*. Seattle: University of Washington Press, 1973.

Kelley, Robert. *Battling the Inland Sea: Floods, Public Policy, and the Sacramento Valley*. Berkeley and Los Angeles: University of California Press, 1989.

Larson, Suzanne B. *"Dig the Ditch!": The History of the Lake Washington Ship Canal*. Boulder, CO: Western Interstate Commission for Higher Education, 1975.

Lonnquest, John, Burt Toussaint, Joe Manous Jr., and Maurits Ertsen, eds. *Two Centuries of Experience in Water-Resources Management: A Dutch-U.S. Retrospective*. Alexandria, VA: Institute for Water Resources, U.S. Army Corps of Engineers and Rijkswaterstaat, Ministry of Infrastructure and the Environment, 2014.

Rogers, Robert P. *An Economic History of the American Steel Industry*. New York: Routledge, 2009.

Thrush, Coll. *Native Seattle: Histories from the Crossing-Over Place*. Seattle: University of Washington Press, 2007.

Williams, David B. *Too High and Too Steep: Reshaping Seattle's Topography*. Seattle: University of Washington Press, 2015.

Willingham, William F. *Northwest Passages: A History of the Seattle District, U.S. Army Corps of Engineers, 1896-1920*. U.S. Army Corps of Engineers, Seattle District, 1992.

LEGISLATION AND COURT CASES

William L. Bilger et al. v. State of Washington, 63 Wash. 457, 116 Pac. 19 (1911).

E. F. Blaine et al. v. M. L. Hamilton et al., 64 Wash. 353, 116 Pac. 1076 (1911).

City of Seattle Ordinance No. 7721, "An ordinance authorizing and directing the Board of Public Works to contract for the sale of Surplus Water to the Seattle and Lake Washington Waterway Co, at a special rate," passed February 3, 1902.

City of Seattle, Ordinance No. 11096, "An Ordinance repealing Ordinance No. 7721, entitled, 'An Ordinance authorizing and directing the Board of Public Works to contract for the sale of surplus water to the Seattle and Lake Washington Waterway Company at a special rate,' approved February 6th, 1902, and directing the Board of Public Works to serve notice upon the said Seattle and Lake Washington Waterway Company that no more water will be supplied said company from and after the 13th day of June, 1904," passed July 18, 1904.

Hewitt-Lea Lumber Company v. King County, 257 U.S. 622, 42 S. Ct. 186, 66 L.Ed.

Laws of Washington 1901, Chapter 6, Construction, Maintenance and Operation of Ship Canal.

Laws of Washington 1907, Chapter 3, Providing for the Sale of Certain Shore Lands and Creating Alaska-Yukon-Pacific Exposition Fund.

Laws of Washington 1909, Chapter 218, Creating a Shore Land Improvement Fund.

Laws of Washington 1909, Chapter 236, Appropriation for State Roads.

River and Harbor Act of 1902, 57th Congress, 1st Session, Chapter 1079.

MANUSCRIPTS AND ARCHIVAL COLLECTIONS

Clarence Bagley Papers. Access. No. 0036-001, University of Washington Special Collections.

Thomas Burke Papers. Access. No. 1483-002, University of Washington Special Collections.

"Correspondence and Papers on the Location and Development of the Lake Washington Canal." Hugh and Jane Ferguson Seattle Room, Seattle Public Library.

Correspondence re: Seattle Garden Club beautification projects, 1971. Folder 30, Box 16, Park Superintendent's Subject Files, 5802-01, Seattle Municipal Archives.

George F. Cotterill Papers. Access. No. 0038-001, University of Washington Special Collections.

Daniel H. Gilman Papers. Access. No. 2730-001, University of Washington Special Collections.

Willard G. Jue Papers. Access. No. 5191-001, University of Washington Special Collections.

Lake Washington Ship Canal, 1916-1951. Water Department Central Files, Record Series 8200-05, Seattle Municipal Archives.

John J. McGilvra Papers. Access. No. 4806-001, University of Washington Special Collections.

John C. Olmsted to Daniel Jones, November 28, 1906. Job 3209, Olmsted Project Records, Washington State Digital Archives.

Records of the Office of the Chief of Engineers, Seattle District. Record Group 77, National Archives and Records Administration, Seattle, Washington.

Eugene Semple Papers. Access. No. 0532-001, University of Washington Special Collections.

Watson C. Squire Papers. Access. No. 4004-002, University of Washington Special Collections.

NEWSPAPERS

The *Seattle Times* and *Seattle Post-Intelligencer* (both searchable online) provided consistent and extensive reporting throughout the history of the canal. Other sources included the *Seattle Gazette*, *Seattle Republican, Seattle Star, Washington Standard*, *Town Crier*, and *Ballard News* and *Seattle Weekly News*.

ONLINE RESOURCES

Troost, Kathy Goetz. *Geomorphology and Shoreline History of Lake Washington, Union Bay, and Portage Bay Technical Memorandum*. Washington State Department of Transportation SR 520, I-5 to Medina: Bridge Replacement and HOV Project website, accessed October 11, 2016: https://www.wsdot.wa.gov/NR/rdonlyres/6ADE9650-8EAF-474B-B38B-6AE3D69242EA/0/SR520_Geomorphology Report_Final_Aug2011_Part1.pdf.

"The U.S. Army Corps of Engineers: A Brief History." U.S. Army Corps of Engineers website, accessed September 10, 2016: http://www.usace.army.mil/About/History/Brief-History-of-the-Corps/Improving-Transportation.

REPORTS

48th Congress, 1st Session. Senate Report No. 494, "On Bill (S1202) to Provide For and Aid in The Construction and to Regulate Operations on a Ship-Canal in Washington Territory," 1884.

52nd Congress, 1st Session. House Exec. Doc. 40, "Canal Connecting Lakes Union, Samamish, and Washington with Puget Sound, Washington," 1892.

54th Congress, 2nd Session. Document No. 2, Volume II, Part 5, "Improvement of Waterway Connecting Puget Sound with Lakes Union and Washington," 1895.

60th Congress, 1st Session. House Doc. No. 953, "Survey of Waterways Connecting Puget Sound with Lakes Union and Washington," 1908.

64th Congress, 1st Session. House Doc. 800, "Lake Washington, Ship Canal, Wash.," 1916.

Annual Report of the Chief of Engineers, 1870-1934.

Annual Report of the Chief of Engineers on Civil Works Activities, 1971-1995.

Beyers, William B., and Richard S. Conway Jr. *The Economic Characteristics of the North Seattle Industrial Area*. Seattle: University of Washington Department of Geography, North Seattle Industrial Association, Neighborhood Business Council, 1991.

Bulletin. Seattle: Port of Seattle Commission, 1912-1916.

Chittenden, H. M. "The Lake Washington Canal: What It Will Mean to the People," [1910?]. Hugh and Jane Ferguson Seattle Room, Seattle Public Library.

Chittenden, Hiram M. *Report of an Investigation by a Board of Engineers of the Means of Controlling Floods in the Duwamish-Puyallup Valleys and Their Tributaries*. Seattle: Lowman and Hanford, 1907.

Commissioner of Public Lands, State of Washington. *Biennial Reports*, 1896-1904.

Environmental Assessment: Lake Washington Ship Canal O&M and Proposed Fish Ladder Improvements. Seattle: Department of the Army, Corps of Engineers, [1971?].

History and Advantages of the Canal and Harbor Improvement Project Now Being Executed by the Seattle and Lake Washington Waterway Company. Seattle: [Seattle and Lake Washington Waterway Company?], 1902.

"Lake Union and the Ship Canal Issues and Opportunities: Background Report and Policy Analysis." Seattle: [Office for Long-Range Planning?], 1989.

Lake Union Study. Seattle: Seattle City Planning Commission, 1963.

Lake Washington After Action Report – 1982. Seattle: Army Corps of Engineers, Seattle District, 1982.

"Lake Washington Ship Canal: Master Plan, Design Memorandum 5." Seattle: Army Corps of Engineers, Seattle District, 1977.

Lake Washington Ship Canal Project. Seattle: Army Corps of Engineers, Seattle District, 1989, Item 5594, Seattle Municipal Archives.

"Naval Reserve Armory." National Register of Historic Places Registration Form, May 27, 2009.

Semple, Eugene. "Financial Proposition for Lake Washington Waterway," July 16, 1893. Folder 3, Box 17, Eugene Semple Papers, 0532-001, University of Washington Special Collections.

Semple, Eugene. "Proposition for a Ship and Water Power Canal Between Elliott Bay and Lake Washington, Near Seattle, Wash," January 3, 1891. Folder 3, Box 17, Eugene Semple Papers, 0532-001, University of Washington Special Collections.

Shoreline Master Program: As Adopted by the City Council, City of Seattle Pursuant to the Shoreline Management Act of 1971, As Amended. Seattle: [City of Seattle?], 1976.

Tobin, Caroline C. *Lake Union and Ship Canal Historical Use Study*. Seattle: Land Use & Transportation Project, 1986.

THESIS

McConaghy, Lorraine Claire Giroux. "The Lake Washington Shipyards: For the Duration." M.A. thesis, University of Washington, 1987.

The *W. T. Preston* moored at the locks, circa 1940s.

PHOTO CREDITS

All images courtesy of Army Corps of Engineers and Friends of the Ballard Locks except where indicated:

6: Library of Congress, Geography and Map Division

9: University of Washington Libraries, Special Collections, POR393

10: Library of Congress, Prints & Photographs Division, Detroit Publishing Company Collection, LC-DIG-det-4a26912

11: Seattle Municipal Archives, 10507

12a: White River Valley Museum

12b: U.S. Army Corps of Engineers

16: Andrew Buchanan/SLP

17: Josef Scaylea, Washington State Digital Archives

18: Library of Congress, Geography and Map Division

20: Courtesy Washington Geological Survey, modified from Patrick Pringle

21: University of Washington Libraries, Special Collections, SEA5735

22: Seattle Municipal Archives, 29524

28: MOHAI, 2002.50.169

31: Seattle Municipal Archives, 70343

32a: Burke Museum

32b: MOHAI, shs7338

33a: Burke Museum

33b: Paul Dorpat

36: Seattle Public Library

38b: MOHAI, 2002.3.437

39: MOHAI, PEMCO Webster & Stevens Collections, 1983.10.6113

40: Library of Congress, Geography and Map Division

42: University of Washington Libraries, Special Collections, A. Curtis 59756

44: MOHAI, shs1152

45: University of Washington Libraries, Special Collections, SEA1097

46: Courtesy Paul Dorpat

47a: MOHAI, 91.5.14

47b: MOHAI, 91.5.12

50-51: University of Washington Libraries, Special Collections, PPC099

52: University of Washington Libraries, Special Collections, SEA1372

53: University of Washington Libraries, Special Collections, POR1212

54: "The Seattle Canal and Land Reclamation Enterprise," *Engineering Record* 32, No. 11 (October 19, 1895), pg. 363

56a: MOHAI, shs 120

56b: University of Washington Libraries, Special Collections, POR882

56c: University of Washington Libraries, Special Collections, POR1991

57: Smyth, W. H., "Hydraulic Dredging: Its Origin, Growth, and Present Status," Proceedings of the Association of Engineering Societies XIX, no. 4, October 1897, 140-163

59: University of Washington Libraries, Special Collections, MAP118

60: University of Washington Libraries, Special Collections, A. Curtis 06577

62: Seattle Municipal Archives

63: University of Washington Libraries, Special Collections, SEA1082

65a: University of Washington Libraries, Special Collections, POR0022

66: Seattle Municipal Archives, 30032

67: Seattle Municipal Archives, 51845

68: Courtesy Paul Dorpat

72a: Courtesy Ron Edge

74: MOHAI, PEMCO Webster & Stevens Collection, 1983.10.9810.1

75b: Seattle Municipal Archives, 100

77: MOHAI, PEMCO Webster & Stevens Collection, 1983.10.6809

78: Seattle Municipal Archives, 6498

79: Courtesy the Bannister Family

83-84: U.S. Army Corps of Engineers

86: MOHAI, 15455

94: MOHAI, PEMCO Webster & Stevens Collection, 1983.10.10325

95a-c: MOHAI, PEMCO Webster & Stevens Collection, 1983

96: U.S. Army Corps of Engineers

97: MOHAI, PEMCO Webster & Stevens Collection, 1983.10.8867

102b: MOHAI, PEMCO Webster & Stevens Collection, 1983.10.3974

103: The Puget Sound Maritime Historical Society

105: Seattle Municipal Archives, 10525

107a: Renton History Museum, 1990.085.3048

108a: Seattle Municipal Archives, 29548

108b: Seattle Municipal Archives, 51954

111a: University of Washington Libraries, Special Collections, UW 38016

111b: The Puget Sound Maritime Historical Society

116a: Courtesy Paul Dorpat

116b: Seattle Municipal Archives, 12846

117a: MOHAI, 2002.48.906

117b: Burke Museum

120: Petyr Beck

121a: The Boeing Company

121b: University of Washington Libraries, Special Collections, UW 19075z

122: University of Washington Libraries, Special Collections, WAS0633

123: Renton History Museum, 1994.068.3883

125: U.S. Army Corps of Engineers

126: Courtesy Vaun Raymond

127: MOHAI, PEMCO Webster & Stevens Collection, 1983.10.9067

135a: Nordic Heritage Museum Collection

135b: Seattle Municipal Archives, 12506

137: Renton History Museum, 41.0322

138a: Terry Donnelly / Alamy Stock Photo

138b: Courtesy Dan Kerlee

141: University of Washington Libraries, Special Collections, UW 6087

145: Mark Summerfield / Alamy Stock Photo

146b: Washington State Department of Transportation

147: Seattle Municipal Archives, 131567

149: Lara Swimmer

151, bottom: Lara Swimmer

160: Lara Swimmer

Back Flap: Lara Swimmer

INDEX

Note: Page numbers in *italic* indicate photographs.

Alexander, Alvin B., 122-123
Alexander, Barton S., 41-42, 48
Alexander, Joseph B., 69
Anaconda (dredger), 57
Army Corps of Engineers, *12-13*, 14, 23, 41, 43, 61, 63, 71, 73, 97, 117, 119, 125, 129-131, 135
    master plan (1977), 143, 145

Ballard, 31, 135
Ballard Bridge, 98, *135*
Ballard Commercial Club, 135, 138
Beacon Hill, 52, *54*, 61, 63, 64
Bear Creek, 32
Bigelow, Reuben, 38
Bilger, William L., 73
Black River, 11, 12, 23, 24, 29, 32, 66, 73, 103, 121-122, *123*, 124, 126, 136
Blake, T. A., 38
Board of Engineers, 41, 47, 60, 61, 62-63, 135
boats, 90-91, 103
    first through the locks, 88
    traffic levels, 101, 130, 131, 142, 143, 145
Bowers Dredging Co., 60
Brace, John, 73
Brainerd, Erastus, 9
bridges, 98-99
budgets, 130-131
Buerge, David, 33
Burke, Thomas, 42, 44, 49, 54, 56, 64, 65, 69, 73, 93, 95
Burton, Hiram, 65
businesses, shoreline, 8, 14, 66, 102, 103, 110, 111, 140, 142, 143, 145

canal digging, 45-46, 73, 76, 78, 97
Canal Era, 10-11
canal routes, proposed, 47-48, 52-61
canals
    Massachusetts, 10
    New York, 10-11
    Washington, 134
Captain Burrows resort, 107
cargo volume, 101, 130, 131, 142, 145
Carlson, Robert A., 78

Casey, Thomas, 47
Cavanaugh, James B., 80, 88, 89, 93, 95, 148
Cayton, Horace, 63
Cedar River, 24, 29, 61, 66, 135, 136-137, 145
Chamber of Commerce, 54, 58, 60, 62, 64, 67
channel depth, 130
Chin Gee Hee, 44
Chinese laborers, 44, 45-46
Chittenden, Hiram M., 9, 64, 65-66, 67, 88, 104, 105, 130, 136
Chun Ching Hock, 44
City of Bothell (boat), *116*
City Council, Seattle, 63, 64
Clapp, John M., 46, 47, 75
Clark, Irving C., 135
coal, 38-39
Coast Guard, 109, *131*, 138
cofferdams, 72, 78, 80-81, 83, 92, 93
Columbia City, 108
concrete, 82, 83
Coontz, Captain, 95-96
cost of building locks, 97
Cotterill, George, 69, 73, 96
crew races, 141
Cummings, J. J., 45, 46

dam bursts, 75
Daphnia (water fleas), 125
Davis, John, and Co., 118
Day, Benjamin F., 42
Denny, Arthur, 54
Denny, David, 35, 42, 45, 47
Dent, Major, 95
dredging, 95, 97
Dunlap Slough, 114
Duwamish River, 7, 12, 14, 24, 26, 108, 136
Duwamish tribe, 32, 126, 127

Eastwick, Philip G., 47
Edgewater, 31
Ehrnbeck, Arthur R., 148
electricity, 88
emergency dam, 132-133
English, Carl S., Jr., 138-139, 148
environmental effects, 11, 113-127
Erickson, C. J., 73, 78, *97*
Esperance Sand, 20

Fairchild, John H., 41
Fallgreen, John A., 135
Ferry, Elisha P., 51, 53
Finke, Ralph, 140, 142
fish, 121-125, 140, 144
fish ladders, 124-125, 140, 146

Fishermen's Terminal, 17, 102, 104-106, *115*, 130, 146
fishing fleet, 8, 17, 102, 104-106, 146
Fishing Vessel Owners Marine Ways, 105
Forrest, William T., 53
Freeman, Miller, 104
Fremont, 31, *49*
Fremont Bridge, *11*, 75, 99
Fremont Cut, 63, 73, 76, *77*, 93, 139, 140, 146
Frye, Charles, 53
Fulton (steamship), 91, 103

gantries, 81, 82, 83
gantry cranes, *70*, 82, 83
Garden Club, Seattle, 139-140
gardens, 138-139
Gardner, Albro, 53
gates, 85, 88, 92
Gilman, Daniel, 49
Gilman, Luthene C., 52
glacier, 19-22
Glenn (freighter), 92
Gould, Carl F., 135, 138
Government Canal, 58, 62, 76
grand opening, 95-96
Graves, Edward O., 54
Great Northern Railway Co., 60, 61, 105
Green River, *12*, 24, 64, 66, 135
Greene, Roger S., 56, 58, 65, 73, 93, 96

Handbury, Thomas H., 41, 47
Harper, Frederick C., 64
Hawley, Dwight S., 138
Hemen, Frank J., 105
Hemlock (lighthouse tender), *15*
Hemrich, Andrew, 53
Hergert, Frank, 47
Heuer, William H., 62
Hewitt-Lea Lumber Co., 107, 118
Hill, James, 49
Hitt, J. M., 9
Holt & Jeffrey, 76
human habitation, earliest, 32-33
Humason, Orlando, 41
Humphrey, William E., 69, 80

King County Board of Commissioners, 54, 64, 69, 136
Kirk, Peter, 39
Klondike Gold Rush, 61-62

Lake Sammamish, 22, 27, 29, 38, 47
Lake Union, 14, 17, 27, 33, 35, 75, 76, 101-102, 130

Lake Washington, 14, *18*, *21*, 22, 23, 33, 35, 108, 110, 125, 126, 131
    formation, 22, 23
    industries, 8, 108, 110
    lowering, 73, 93, 95, 107, 113, 114, 116-124
Lake Washington Canal Association, 65
Lake Washington Improvement Co., 42, 45, 47
Lamont, Daniel S., 58
Landon, Dan, 96
Latona, 31
Laughery, Dail Butler, 122
Lawton Clay, 19-20
Lewarch, Dennis, 32-33
Lidén, Ernst, 87
lighthouses, 109
locks, location of, 66-67, 69
locks, other, 93
logs, transporting, 47, *107*, *118*, 130, 143
lumber mills, 48, *50-51*, 67, 69, 92, 107, 118, 143

Mackenzie, Alexander, 64, 65
Mary Frances (tug), 92
May B II (ferry), 88
McClellan, George B., 9
McConnell, Richard E., *139*
McElroy, James, 96
McEwan, Alexander F., 69
McGilvra, John J., 14, 53-54, 56, 58, 60, 62, 67, 108
McGraw, John, 49, 52, 53, 64, 65, 73
McNaught, James, 41
Meacham & Babcock Shipbuilding, 102, 105
Mendell, George H., 47-48
Mercer Slough, 114, 116, 118
Mercer, Thomas, 7, 32, 35, 36
Mercer's Farm route, 41, 48, *55*
military installations, 109
Miller, Betty, 139
Mississippi Valley Trust Co., 57
Mitchell, John R., 78
Montlake Cut, 63, *78*, *79*, 80, *86*, *92*, 93, *94*, 95, 120, *139*, 141, 145, 146
Montlake dump, 121
Montlake Portage, 27, 46, 47, 63
Moore, James A., 31, 64, 65, 108
Moss Bay Iron and Steel Works, 39

Native Americans, 11, 32-33, 126-127
north canal, 52, 53, 54, 58, 60, 61, 62, 63

oceangoing ships, 103, 106
Olmsted, John Charles, 110
opening day, 95-96

Orcas (boat), *15*, 88, 90, 92-93
Osprey (steamship), 91, 102

parks, 110
Pearson Construction, 80
Perkins, William, 38
Phinney, Guy, 42
Pike, Harvey L., 36, 37, 41
Piles, Samuel H., 67, 76, 96, 100, 130
pintle hinge, 84, 85, 88
pleasure boats, 110-111, 142-143, 145, 146
Pontiac, 31
Port of Seattle Commission, 64, 102, 104, 105, 106, 142, 145
Portage Bay, *8*, 27, 34, *36*, *45*, *46*, 47, *72-73*, 78, 95, 143
Powell, Archibald, 121, 126
Powell, John H., 69
Princess Marguerite (ship), *140*
Puget lobe, 19, 20, 82
Puget (snagboat), *119*
Puget Sound Bridge and Dredging Co., 81

railroads, 38-39, 60, 69
Ravenna, 114, 117, 118, 121
Renton, 114, 118, 121, 136
Ricksecker, Eugene, 46, 54, 67
Robbins, James R., 41
Roosevelt (boat), 90-91, 95, 96
Ross (town), 31
Ross Creek, 27, 123

salmon, 121-125, 136, 140, 146
Salmon Bay, 8, 11, 27, *28*, 48, 61, 66, 92, 102, *108*, *112*, 113-114, 125, *127*, 131
saltwater incursion, 120
Sammamish River, 23, 27, 29, 114
Sargent, Arthur W., 130, 148
Scurry and Snow, 42
sea lions, 144
Seattle Coal & Transportation Co., 38, *40*, 41
Seattle and Lake Washington Waterway Co., 53, 54, 57, 58, 60, 61, 63, 64
Seattle Post-Intelligencer, 60-61
Seattle Times, 60
Seattle and Walla Walla Railroad and Transportation Co., 39
Semple, Eugene, 51-52, 53, 54, 57, 62, 65
Shilshole Bay route, 48, *55*, 58, 61
shipbuilding industry, 102-103
shipworms, 12, 48, 114
Shore Land Improvement Fund, 69
Shoreline Master Program, 143

smelt, 125
Smith Cove route, *55*, 60-61
Smith, E. Victor, 120
Snoqualmie tribe, 32
south canal, 51, 52-54, 57, 58, 60, 62, 63, 64
spillway, 92, 133
Squak Slough, 27, 29, 114, *116*
Squire, Watson, 58, 73, 91
steelhead, 144
Stevens, Isaac I., 9, 134
Stillwell Brothers Construction Co., 78-80, *86*
Stimson, Henry Lewis, 69
Sturtevant, Clark, 116
Suquamish tribe, 32-33, 127
Swinomish (snagboat), 90, 92, 119
Symons, Thomas W., 47, 53, 54, 58, 130

teredos, 48, 114
Thomson, Reginald H., 58, 96
tourists, 135, 138, 140, 146
traffic volume, 101, 130, 131, 142, 143, 145
Tramway route, 41, 48, *55*
trees, submerged, 119
Triton (ferry), 119
tugboats, 103, *107*

Union Bay Natural Area, 121
Union City, 37, 41

Venischnick, Ruth, 117

Wa Chong Co., 44, 45-46, 47, 76
water flow into the cuts, 88, 92-93
water levels, 117, 131, 135, 145
wetlands, 114, 116-118, 121, 126
Wetmore Slough, 108, 114, *116*, 121
whalers, 102
White River, *12*, 24, 75
White Sands (dry dock), *128*
White, Will R., 52
Wild, H. J., 97
Williams, Arthur, 75, 78, 148
Willingham, William F., 43, 65
Winters, Frederick, 118
workers, 87
World War I, 102
World War II, 138
W. T. Preston (snagboat), *43*, 90, 156

Yesler, Henry, 7, 31, 45
Yesler (town), 31
Yesler's Wharf, *42*
Young, Charles A. D., 132, 148

The authors explore
one of the culverts
used to fill the large
lock, 2016.